MINGUS/MINGUS

Janet Coleman and Al Young

MINGUS/MINGUS

TWO MEMOIRS

Limelight Editions

NEW YORK

1991

This project could not have been accomplished without the efforts of Susan Berg-holz, Judy Daniels, Donald S. Ellis, Sue Mingus, Peg O'Donnell and Nancy Riddi-ough. The authors also gratefully acknowledge the contributions of Atlantic Records, Red Callender, CBS Records, Sally Coleman, Ted Curson, Diane Dorr-Dorynek, David Dozer, Phil Elwood, Dizzy Gillespie, Robert Gordon, Alex Green, John Handy, Nat Hentoff, Sy Johnson, Louis Kagen, KPFA-Berkeley (Pacifica Foundation), Perry Lederman, Ann McIntosh, Joni Mitchell, Carolyn Mingus, Charles Mingus III, David Newman, Nehemiah Pitts, Max Roach, Cheri Stein Sandweiss, Jill Sheinberg, Mark Silber, Edmund White, Robert Ungaro, Susanna Ungaro, Arl Young and Celia Mingus Zaentz.

Portions of this book, in slightly different form, have appeared in *Fame*.

First Limelight Edition October 1991

Library of Congress Cataloging-in-Publication Data
Coleman, Janet, 1942–
    Mingus/Mingus: two memoirs/Janet Coleman and Al Young.—1st Limelight ed.
        p. cm.
    Originally published: Berkeley: Creative Arts Book Co., 1989.
    ISBN 0–87910–149–0
    1. Mingus, Charles, 1922– . 2. Coleman, Janet, 1942– .
3. Young, Al, 1939– . 4. Jazz musicians—United States—Biography. I.
Young, Al, 1939– Mingus/Mingus. 1991.
II. Title.
[ML418.M45C6 1991]   91–23247   CIP   MN
781.65′092—dc20
[B]

MINGUS/MINGUS

Janet Coleman

I knew Charles Mingus almost twenty years, in various cities, at various weights, in canny and uncanny moments, and through various psychic and aesthetic incarnations: I bore witness to his Shotgun, Bicycle, Camera, Witchcraft, Cuban Cigar and Juice Bar periods, and was familiar with his Afro, Egyptian, English banker, Abercrombie and Fitch, Sanford and Son, and ski bunny costumes. I ate his chicken and dumplings, kidneys and brandy, popcorn and garlic, pigs, rabbits, godknows mice.

I met him when I was a college student in Ann Arbor. He was playing at a jazz club in Detroit, the Minor Key. He saw I was white. He guessed I was Jewish. He told his sideman, Booker Ervin, not to hit on me. We had a correspondence. Back in New York on school vacations, I came to know the various branches of the Mingus dynasty: children, stepchildren, wives, ex-wives, friends, musicians, cronies. Once when Mingus thought a friend had fed him poisoned dinner, he drank a glass of olive oil as an antidote. I missed that event. But I saw him drink a glass of cream.

He was not a person to be taken lightly, either as a musician or as a man. He was a reigning genius of jazz, an oil well of musical accomplishment. He played with everyone from Kid Ory to Lionel Hampton to Charlie Parker. He plowed every musical root and tradition from Natchez to Salzburg and wherever the four winds ever blew. On the bass he was a virtuoso. He was the molder and mastermind of the various bands and ensembles that performed under the aegis of the Charles Mingus Jazz Workshop (or Sweatshop, according to some musicians who played in them). The final one was a quintet. He created a body of music so rich and moving, complex and original, that when Mingus was forty-eight, Whitney Balliett said his compositions "may equal anything written in Western music in the past twenty years." As a composer he ranks with his idol, Duke Ellington, for having stretched the canvas and palette of jazz to the point where it transforms from tunes and jamming into the realm that Rahsaan Roland Kirk called "black classical music." ("Jazz is only a word and really has no meaning," Duke Ellington said. "We stopped using it in 1943.")

Mingus thought of himself primarily as a composer. But he was also a pioneer in applying jazz concepts to other art forms: theater, painting, poetry, ballet. He composed for Alvin Ailey. John Cassavetes' first improvised movie, *Shadows*, had a Mingus score. He and Max Roach were the first jazz musicians to create and market records on their own label (Debut), and, thanks to Mingus's diligence as an archivist, we have the famous *Jazz at Massey Hall* album, one of the last recorded meetings of the bebop greats of the 1940s. Mingus also published numerous pamphlets, manifestos and diatribes (e.g., "To John 'Ass' Wilson of the *New York Times*"), and wrote at least as many liner notes for his own record albums as Nat Hentoff. "The Charles Mingus CAT-a-logue for Toilet Training Your Cat" ("Don't be surprised if you hear the toilet flush in the middle of the night. A cat can learn how to do it, spurred on by his instinct to cover up. His main thing is to cover up.") used to be available for a dollar at a post office box at Cooper Station, New York, NY 10003.

I sensed the breadth of Mingus's extra-musical abilities the first time I visited him in New York, in 1960. He was living with his fourth wife Judy in the Lenox Towers, on 135th Street in Harlem. I was eighteen and I brought along my best friend, Patty Sexton, a teenaged socialist, composer of the song, "I Love You, Vladimir." That night Judy was in the hospital, giving birth to their daughter Carolyn. Mingus was in the kitchen, cooking up a batch of chicken and dumplings. He sat us at the kitchen table, fed us and thought of sending flowers to his wife. He called the florist and then pulled out several reams of manuscript. Judy had been typing it. It was Mingus's book, named either *Half Yaller Nigger* or *Half Yaller Schitt-Colored Nigger*, he hadn't decided which yet, though he was pretty sure no white man would let him use any of those words in print. And so he had a safety title too, *Beneath the Underdog*, the social situation in America, he explained, of a half-yaller schitt-colored nigger.

My friend and I read the manuscript into the night. We were amazed. It was a jumble, a torrent, it was like James Joyce, jazzy Joyce, and it was terrific. It had puns and wordplay, and a schizophrenic narrator, Baby A and Baby B.

At 7:00 A.M. he thought I ought to call my mother, so she wouldn't worry, and invited me to edit it.

Al Young says Mingus offered him the same job "ten minutes after I met him." They were on the steps of the Showplace, a small and, during the nine-month residence of the Jazz Workshop, an intensely charged nightclub on West Fourth Street in Greenwich Village. "He wanted me to help him because I knew about his music and because he thought I was more educated than he was. I could write in sentences and stuff."

I wasn't much of an editor: I liked Mingus's book exactly as it was. Nevertheless, I left with sheaves of his most recent inserts, written in hand, on yellow legal pads. In a follow-up letter that promised even more material, he wrote that he was

> . . . concerned as of your opinion as far as: Does it sound clear? Does the writer sound convincing? Has he been dead and alive?

❖   ❖   ❖

IT MAY ILLUMINATE THE JAZZ-FAN SOCIOLOGY of the period to mention that Al Young and I were both, at that time, beatniks and English majors at the University of Michigan. Al was also a performer, a singer, a very good one, who seemed to shun an almost certain future as a popular black star, to protect his life as a writer, a rather high-minded decision. (He could have been a sex symbol.) He met Mingus a few months before I did, under similar circumstances, at a jazz club in a city he was passing through. (Al was from Detroit.) Our friend Ann McIntosh met Mingus even earlier, and appears briefly in *Beneath the Underdog* as the post-debutante from Vassar that she was before she came to Ann Arbor and put on black tights. The coincidence of us three knowing him never seemed remarkable to Mingus, nor did the fact that we seemed to turn up everywhere.

Mingus, at the time, was very much the author.

_____ 5

After the brilliant run of his Jazz Workshop at the Showplace, he wrote me that he viewed its unemployment as "a chance to write about the true jazz scene that has made our *masters* millions and taken the most famed to their penniless graves they had awaited as the only escape from the invisible chains on black jazz as an art." On the next page, he reminded me that he felt "pressed to make each written word count for my book." And on the next page, he regretted "the pages I should cover with ink in my attempt to write a book that will survive me. Each moment of cramping my hand I feel must be used with thought in mind . . . this is my pick and shovel, novel." It occurred to him that "maybe you'll have a book called *Letters to and from Mingus*" on the third P.S.

Al Young remembers Mingus keeping him posted on the progress of the book in various places around the country. "I'm workin' on a new chapter now. It's in my head," he had started to say. "I think when I told him I was a writer, he decided I would steal it," Al Young says.

I didn't want to be a writer. I put *Half Yaller Nigger* on my resume, and Erika Munk hired me to do subscriptions at the *Partisan Review*. It was more like a city college faculty lounge in 1937 than a job. I was twenty. I lived in a 100-year-old furnished room on Christopher Street, around the corner from the Ninth Circle, a great Village bar owned by Bobby Krivit and Mickey Ruskin, before Mickey went on alone to create a succession of great Village bars all over Manhattan, including Max's Kansas City.

Judy Mingus, previously a nurse from Yonkers, was around twenty-five, a sweet and gentle girl, strawberry blonde, disowned by her family and pregnant again when Mingus started coming downtown all the time, complaining he was lonely. I had an on-and-off-again affair with a graduate student in Rhode Island, suitably defined by my bioenergetic psychiatrist as "pathological." I took Mingus to the Ninth Circle to cheer myself up. I went there every single night.

Among the pleasures of the Ninth Circle were a jazz jukebox, integrated barflys, lightning fast jive Ping-Pong between the bartenders, James "Snooky" Nazarro and Robert "Shoupy" Shoup, Mickey's trademark pumpernickel, an emotionally explosive atmosphere, and peanuts in shells you dropped on the floor. Mingus took to it, "the peanut bar," and soon he was one of its outstanding features. It was the speed of his reflexes toward the kitchen to get the butcher knife that turned Mingus's racial imbroglio with a famous drinker, Dan McCabe, into a Village legend. Mingus had a rapport with Bobby Krivit, based primarily on their large sizes, and it was testy only when one of them was on a diet. He entrusted Krivit with safekeeping huge cash payrolls, which he transported from nightclub gigs to the Ninth Circle in his socks.

In the square world I worked in, publishing, the

Mingus manuscript was something of a special curio or jewel. McGraw-Hill had it under option for quite a while, and there was a succession of ambitious young male editors. Some of them were black. Whenever there was a possibility for publication, Mingus seemed to balk. Jason Epstein, the big kingpin at Random House, was interested in the manuscript until he heard a few of Mingus's conditions: a white binding with gold letters, a book that could be mistaken for the Bible. Well, fuck him, Jason Epstein said. It is hard to estimate how many people finally worked on the copy, hacks and strangers, people who appealed to the author (and his various editors) because they could spell. I saw it once again in 1965 or 1966, and even then, before it reached its last editor, Nel King, it had been altered, whitened up beyond repair. *Beneath the Underdog* was published in 1971 by Alfred A. Knopf, without the gold lettering, weak tea indeed. It managed, however, to set down some autobiographical record, and to preserve Mingus's original spelling of "schitt."

❖   ❖   ❖

MINGUS WAS BORN IN AN ARMY CAMP in Nogales, Arizona, April 22, 1922. (According to him and one of his occult sources, the preponderance of twos was a numerological phenomenon.) He grew up in Watts, California. His father gave him his first instrument to play, a trombone, at the age of six. It is obvious that he showed himself at once as a musical prodigy, though his talents were rewarded rather differently from, let's say, Mozart's. He was taught, like most poor black children, by an itinerant music teacher, who found it easier to teach the pupils how to play by the finger and ear method than how to read music. This early inability to read, he said, was a source of great humiliation, and retarded his classical training by several years, during which time he learned, of course, to improvise. In high school he was playing cello with the Los Angeles Junior Philharmonic, but on the advice of his friend, Buddy Collette, he traded in the cello for a "Negro instrument," the double bass. "You can't slap a cello, Charlie," Collette said, "so you gotta learn to slap that bass." He learned everything else about the bass as well, studying first with Red Callender, and later with M. Reinschaugen, the principal bassist of the New York Philharmonic. He practiced fingering for hours, training the rarely used fourth finger to become his own most agile digit. He studied composition with Lloyd Reese.

Having driven himself so hard to acquire the technical skills white people seemed to inherit so casually, he was chronically horrified by negligent craftsmanship.

In 1974, listening with him, before a concert, to his old recordings, I watch the chef recook his stew. He sits directly in front of the record player, hands folded on his Buddha-belly. Mingus's belly prevails, no matter what diets, pills, fasts and regimens he subjects it to. He is dressed in a pair of huge black Vietcong-style pajamas he designed himself. His beard and sideburns are flecked with gray now, and his hair grows in an unmanicured, unruly Afro. On occasion he has shaved it off. He has a beautiful face. Mingus's eyes, whether pleased or angry, hooded with suspicion or lit with delight, register his feelings so intensely he can alter the magnetic balance of a room.

He is an avid, noisy audience, talking back to the records, chiding or approving the musicians, remembering each moment of performance as he hears it back. On *Mingus at Monterey* there is a long bowed solo on the bass. "That sound in tune to you?" he asks. "Sounds sharp to me," he answers. "Sounds like I'm playing sharp *all* the time. My singing teacher told us you should do that. Maybe I got it from her. She said singers when they grow old have a tendency to go flat. So if you sing sharp as a young person, as you get older and go flat, you'll be in tune. In other words, it's never thought good to be flat," he says. "It means you can't get to the tone." He nods and sings with Jaki Byard's piano solo ("He knows just what to play. Peeta, *peeta* peeta pu!"). On the record, Mingus answers Byard on the bass. In person he reviews his own solo: "I guess people don't applaud that shit. The stuff I'm doin' now." Buddy Collette comes in on flute. "That's Buddy," Mingus says. "Buddy's a master flute player. Watch

him play." There is applause on the record for
Buddy Collette. "He's the only one who got applause," Mingus observes, more surprised than
envious of his old friend. Translating his own next
solo, Mingus, in person, sings along, an adoring
father cooing through the slots of a crib: "Do you
hear me talkin' to you, Buddy? Do you hear me,
Buddy?" "Much better," he comments on his second
turn. "Thass *bad!*" As the chorus comes in, Mingus
recapitulates the events at Monterey: "McPherson,
see, he's helpin'. Dannie's responsible for that. He's
bad! He's conducting the band!" Then, on the record, there is tumultuous applause and crowds of
people shouting. From the cacophony of audience
sounds at Monterey, Mingus singles out Jaki Byard's
voice. "All right, Chazz!" he thinks he hears, and
plays that portion of the record back again.

He chooses another version of the same tune
next, an earlier one, recorded at an uptown club.
Here, Eric Dolphy, ten years dead, the namesake of
Mingus's youngest son, is playing on the flute. "Uh-
oh," says Mingus, admonishing the dead man,
"Eric's out of tune. He plays like a kid compared to
Buddy. He hasn't mastered his instrument."

❖   ❖   ❖

"PEOPLE DON'T KNOW WHAT IT TOOK to be a jazz
musician," Mingus often said. If you have ever

heard the Japanese play jazz, you know that technique and persistence are not alone the qualities it takes. "Jazz is nigger music," Mingus, grimly, would always say. He trained his own ear on Beethoven, Bartok, Stravinsky, Richard Straus ("Ri*chard* Straus. The one who wrote 'Death and Transfiguration,' not the one who wrote Viennese waltzes.") and Orson Welles ("I dug his voice. It reminded me of Coleman Hawkins. You could hear it a mile away."). But his earliest and deepest musical influences were "Duke Ellington records on radio" and his stepmother's Holiness Church, where they sang and swooned and carried on. (His father, who was so light-skinned a Negro that in his Army photograph he appears to be the only white man in the ranks, was more "assimilated" than the stepmother and was a Methodist. He sternly disapproved of orgiastic church behavior and also of the radio.)

The church meeting tradition—of spontaneous group participation—remained the juice for all of Mingus's work. ("Jazz is improvisation," Mingus said. "Improvisation is jazz.") He made the distinction between himself and "pencil" composers because he intended his music to be played by a community of musicians who shared both jazz traditions and technical discipline to such a degree that they could improvise their own musical visions and opinions within the framework of even the most complex composition.

Mingus's career blossomed in the late forties in

just such a community, among the beboppers, then creating a musical revolution, bringing to jazz technical and conceptual innovation as complex and serious as the most "serious" modern music. Duke Ellington called it "*un climat extraordinaire.*" The new sounds reached Mingus in California via touring musicians, and in 1951 he moved to New York to join a rare constellation of musical giants, including Bud Powell, Dizzy Gillespie, Thelonious Monk and Charlie Parker, Bird, who was not only the most brilliant player, but also seems to have been the most inspirational and benevolent spirit, practically a saint.

Charlie Parker's effect on Mingus was profound. In the notes to *Mingus Dynasty*, Mingus wrote that "Bird brought to music a primitive, mystic, supramind communication that I'd only heard in the late Beethoven quartets, and, even more, in Stravinsky." In a less erudite mood he once told me, "Bird was an ESP man. He knows what you're thinkin'. 'Don't take that next breath.' Bird would say something like that. He was a very educated man. Self-educated probably. I don't think he went to college. But he could talk on any subject. He'd talk to doctors. He'd talk about isotopes, frontal lobotomies, all kinds of shit. To cure himself of drugs. He was very religious. He said he knew when he was going to die. It ain't like it used to be. The guys aren't together. They're all separated. Individuals now. Bird was a symbol. It was a clique, a clique of people.

Who all believed in one thing: gettin' high. And playin'."

That pure idea was complicated, however, by the fact that they were black. For all their antics, "cool" philosophy, dark glasses and goatees, the beboppers were the first wave of black jazzmen to see themselves not as just entertainers and showmen, but as musicians and as artists. "God, they were an arrogant group," Al Young recollects. They were the darlings of the educated and moneyed elite, hero-worshiped and emulated in the subterranean haunts of the first group, partied and seduced in the mansions of the second.

But they were also ostracized by the jazz establishment, the big booking agencies and the big recording companies. In a business situation, the beboppers were too much trouble, prima donnas. It was easier to copy what they were doing, in diluted white versions that would sell. Among many of the successful black old-timers, they were another kind of threat: Louis Armstrong (who was "owned," like a boxer, by a white manager, Joe Glaser) recorded a version of the "Wiffenpoof Song" and aimed the sarcasm at their music: "Poor little lambs with their flatted fifths, baa, baa, baa."

Squeezed out into the fringes of the marketplace, many of these musicians died young, poor, disillusioned, addicted. The survivors grew wary and bitter. The Massey Hall session, for example, recorded shortly after Bud Powell's discharge from a mental hospital, and only two years before the death of Charlie Parker, was a producer's nightmare of personality clashes and frayed nerves. That Mingus persisted in doing it at all is testimony to his sense of obligation to this period of jazz history.

He never made peace with himself about it. As if his memory kept turning up the fragments of an unsolved puzzle, he would offer up odd bits of gossip about the financial misfortunes, aborted careers, compromised or shattered lives of other jazz musicians he had once considered great.

It is a summer night in 1974. Sitting around the big wooden table at the floor-through on East Tenth Street where Mingus lives, we are comparing Demeara Lemon Hart to Mount Gay Rum. The two kinds of rum are augmented by three kinds of coke. Mingus is discussing one of his favorite subjects, the unequal distribution of wealth to jazz musicians. He has experienced eclipses in his own career, but not this year. He has just signed a new contract with Atlantic Records, and he is peeling an avocado with great dexterity, using a Swiss Army knife. "Most of the classical soloists, they live good, they ride around in Rolls Royces. Most of 'em marry very wealthy women. Or have a sponsor," Mingus says.

I ask him if the Newport fans had ever served as patrons. "They just gave parties," Mingus says. "Although someone must have been sponsoring Willie the Lion. 'Cause I never knew where he was workin'." He is sweeping the avocado peels into an empty grocery bag when a new drift of memory reminds him that one baroness's financial aid to various musicians extended only for their drugs. "She could have set a nightclub up. She could have set up concerts. Somethin' wrong with her. She must be crazy. She could have set Bird up in a position as prominent as Duke Ellington, as far as making a living was concerned." Mingus whacks apart the avocado. "If art was show business, Charlie Parker would be a millionaire." Mingus sighs. "Pass the coke," he says.

For all his trials as Mingus's friend, critic and arranger, Sy Johnson is pre-eminent among the "Mingusologists." He says of this particular obsession, "It was Charles' star-crossed time."

❖   ❖   ❖

MINGUS WENT ON TO DEFINE his own musical voice apart from "The Cool School," the other descendants of bebop. Steeped as it is in church music and the blues, and infused also with romantic Ellingtonian melodies, Mingus's music is anything but cool.

I first heard it when I was in high school, late at night on the radio, waiting for Symphony Sid to play my request ("Speak Low," as sung, spectacularly, by Sarah Vaughan). I come from a family of expressive Jewish talkers, but I had never heard such drama, such story-telling, such a wide range of feeling and ideas, expressed in sound before.

Mingus music is turbulent, lyrical, raucous, funny, witty, unpredictable and oceanic. It unfolds through constantly transforming rhythms: African, Latin, Indian, waltz, blues. The arrangements are embroidered lavishly with threads from a vast musical memory: chanting, singing, clapping, moaning, Wagnerian motifs, a phrase from Mozart's "Horn Concerto" (played backward), a snatch of "Tea for Two." Arranging for Mingus, Sy Johnson learned that some of the pyrotechnical razzle-dazzle was actually Mingus's device for concealing, or, in his mind, patenting the classical bedrock beneath it. "I don't want anyone findin' out my shit, man," Mingus said.

Mingus seemed to extract an enormous richness and variety of sound from small ensembles, but in fact the bigger the band, the better it did his music justice. Like most jazz innovators of the fifties, however, he worked in small clubs, and too erratically to maintain a big payroll of veteran musicians. It became his custom to hire young ones.

Working for Mingus, Ted Curson once said, was "definitely a university thing." He was widely recognized as a teacher, and besides Curson, Mingus's roster of Jazz Workshop scholars included Booker Ervin, Eric Dolphy, John Handy, Charles McPherson, Jackie McLean, Jon Faddis, Don Pullen, Jaki Byard, Roland Kirk, Yusef Lateef, Jimmy Knepper and his most important musical connection, the drummer Sy Johnson refers to as "the other half of

Mingus's heartbeat," Dannie Richmond. (Dannie played with Mingus from 1956—when he was twenty-one and had been playing drums six months—to 1978, longer than anyone, most of twenty-two years.) They have all attested that, in one way or another, Mingus turned their heads around. In a Mingus operation, "Mingus was the boss. He gave the orders. He was the musical director, and he had ideas on everything," Ted Curson said.

With every new Jazz Workshop ensemble, Mingus's unannounced ambition was to train musicians to perform his music with the artistry—and fraternity—of Charlie Parker. In his opinion, they hardly ever did.

This crop of new kids, they can't play together. They all want to be stars. Without any roots, without any background, without any of the past touching them. None of the guys in my band can play anything that Bird's played. Not one of his solos. They're not capable. They haven't practiced what the masters left for them.

There are some guys playin' the saxophone who'd *quit* if they heard Coleman Hawkins. They have to play on microphones. Ben Webster and Coleman Hawkins came up at a time when there were no mikes. They had to use big loud sounds. *Tones*. Beautiful loud *tones*. That carried all over the outdoors.

When all these guys go up to the mike to play, they don't move me at all. I can't hear. My guys put mikes in their horns. Yeah, my men do. Ornette Coleman does it too.

"Mingus is a super bebopper," Dizzy Gillespie once told me, not unmischievously. "Every trumpet he get, he sound like me; every saxophone he get, he sound like Yardbird. He's a super bebopper." As both a founding father and sturdy survivor of bebop—a grand master—Dizzy is giving here the kind of appraisal Mingus usually gives of one of the new crop of kids. "I think one of his main contributions is administration of the music, of putting it together. He reminds me of a young Duke. As a matter of fact, his music sounds like Duke Ellington." Dizzy paused, to let his insight take effect. "I think that's the main thing," he resumed, "his organizational genius." I asked him what about the other things, the way that Mingus played the bass, or how he led a band. "He doesn't play enough," said Dizzy sternly. "You have to play *all* the time," he said. "Sometimes he plays and his fingers start bleedin'." And as a bandleader, "Mingus suffers mostly from a lack of his peers, musicians up to his ability. You have to have musicians who can go in and go 'boom.'" I pointed out to Dizzy that he was one of Mingus's few remaining peers. "He wouldn't be able to pay me," Dizzy said. "Even Duke wouldn't have been able to pay me."

I confronted Sy Johnson (not Mingus) with Dizzy's remarks about the bleeding fingers. "Dizzy doesn't leave anything to chance," Sy Johnson said. "He practices all the time. He's continually keeping his facilities up, like an athlete getting ready. Dizzy expresses himself entirely through the trumpet. Mingus's music is in his head. He ruminates at the piano. He's never been just a bass player. He doesn't think that way."

❖ ❖ ❖

IN EARLY 1963, MINGUS RENTED A LOFT on Third Avenue and Twenty-seventh Street. The answering pick-up was "Music, Art and Health, who's calling?" He was planning a school that would incorporate all the arts in a healthy atmosphere. "I've got a minister, a Zen teacher, Charles Rice, who teaches karate, and Katherine Dunham for dance and witchcraft." Along the entrance wall he envisioned a "juice bar and juice extractor." At the far end, an engineering room. The floor there was hollow. It would stay unfinished until he could afford to lay wires for the recording equipment, "'cause they have to go under the *cee*-ment." He had bags and bags of cement.

Except for a few square holes of missing sound-proofing, the loft's main room was almost finished. It smelled of newly sanded wood and incense. It was very cold and almost empty, except for an upright piano and about fifteen huge pieces of chrome exercise equipment, which looked like salvage from some interplanetary health spa.

Ann McIntosh and I were hostessing a beatnik reunion in New York and brought some girlfriends there one night. Mingus brought out a Chinese water pipe and a big leaf: Persian leaf tobacco, a Mingus discovery, hard to get, but legal.

"It was legal, that was it," Arline Belch, later Al's wife, Arl Young, recalls. "It didn't get us high." I don't remember smoking it. I only remember the scent of incense and how all four of us fell asleep on the slant boards. Some of us were right side up, some were upside down. We fell asleep to the sound of Mingus composing at the piano. In the morning, he took us downstairs to the Greek coffee shop for breakfast. We all sat in a row at the counter and ordered orange juice and doughnuts. "The best part was the way he played the piano. The ethereal quality it had. Which surprised me 'cause I'd only heard him play bass. He was very protective," Arl says, "like we were his daughters. Like a mother singing a lullaby."

The motherly aspect of Mingus's personality never developed at his school. He was evicted from the loft before the floor was finished, for an infraction of the fire laws. When he talked about the project afterward, it was in connection with police payola and how he wasn't smart enough to pay it.

And the next time he was served with eviction papers (from a loft on Great Jones Street), his departure was recorded by a documentary filmmaker and all the New York papers.

On the innocent premise that a mental hospital could help him solve his mental problems, Mingus during the same period had himself committed to Bellevue. In a Catch-22 development, he then could not get out. Even there (to the tune of screaming inmates, a threatened lobotomy and a diagnosis of "Negro, Paranoid"), he tried to organize some patients (a tap dancer, a very famous chess player and himself) into a combine in which they could pool their assorted skills and talents. His request for a blackboard and a workroom was denied. "May I comment," said the doctor, "that compulsive organization is one of the prime traits of paranoia."

If he was often faced with this white diagnosis of his creativity, he was continually organizing life into a nascent state of it. He had a plan to start a ballroom and a ballroom band. He said jazz was routed out of the dance hall and into the nightclub because "dancing was too big a help to integration." Giving his music the dignity it deserved was his recurrent theme. "I wasn't born in a nightclub," he once said.

In 1963, after he recorded *The Black Saint and the Sinner Lady*, a major work (for Impulse), Mingus invited his psychologist, Dr. Edmund Pollock, to share the space with him on the album's liner notes and to review the music. (It had been com-

posed during their therapy.) In his notes Dr. Pollock
tells us that he reacted to Mingus's invitation with
some surprise. "I told him I was competent enough
as a psychologist, but that my interest in music was
only average and without any technical background. Mr. Mingus laughed and said he didn't care,
that if I heard his music I'd understand." Then (as if
his pipe was clenched too tightly in his teeth) Pollock tells us that although his patient is "inarticulate
in words, he is gifted in musical expression, which
he constantly uses to articulate what he perceives
and knows and feels," and warming, begins to ex-
plicate the music. ("There can be no question that
he is the Black Saint who suffers for his sins . . .")

Next is Mingus's own account of the music.

Time, perfect or syncopated time, is when a
faucet dribbles from a leaky washer. I'm more
than sure an adolescent memory can remember
how long the intervals were between each colli-
sion of our short-lived drip and its crash into an
. . . untidy rust-stained enamel sink that the
owner of such has given up on the idea that the
maintenance man is ever going to change the
rhythm beat of his leaking faucet by just doing
his job and changing that rotten old rubber
washer before time runs out of time.

Musicians partly come into the circle of
various blames which encompass much more
than leaky faucets, rotten washers, or critics. _____ 23

| MINGUS | Wow! Critics! How did they get here. I know. It's |
| MINGUS | Freudian. Faucets and old washers. |

One wonders who, in that relationship, was the washer, and who was the faucet.

❖ ❖ ❖

GENIUS ASSERTS ITSELF IN MANY WAYS. Sometimes simply as a special energy, an aura. In jazz it is revealed in live performance. Mingus's could not be beat. He was a natural instinctive actor, a player, a profound photographic study, a born comedian.

Many of Mingus's onstage theatrics have been documented: outbursts on the bandstand, brawls and knife fights, bashing up his bass. Most of these occurrences were intrinsic to the work, musical primal scream sessions in which he, like a Janov of the bass, would drive each musician to connect with his core. At his most explosive, in the Jazz Workshops of the early sixties, "you never knew who was going to be screamed into submission or humiliated, or wooed and loved into playing what Charles wanted him to play," one fan, his fifth wife, Susan Graham Ungaro Mingus, would recall, and not without nostalgia. He might stop a tune in the middle and start it over again. He might hire and fire and rehire a recalcitrant sideman all in a night. "He stopped at nothing to get the quality he wanted. Nothing was too awful, nothing was sacred. And his musicians played their asses off." Some have never stretched themselves so far again. His principle was to learn everything there is to know about your instrument, and then to "play yourself." Mingus would be the judge of how well his musicians accomplished either of these tasks.

Sy Johnson played piano in the Mingus band at the Showplace in 1960 for two weeks. During that run, he remembers Mingus chasing Ted Curson and his trumpet around West Fourth Street once a night, and screaming at Eric Dolphy, "Play with taste, man, play with taste." He shortly tormented the new man, the even-tempered Johnson, into a rage.

"We were playing that tune of his, 'All the Things You Could Be by Now If Sigmund Freud's Wife Was Your Mother.' It was really an obstacle course. There were chromatic changes, Latin rhythms, 6/8 times. You had to fight your way through."

That was the idea. Mingus took pains to sabotage facile performances. For instance, he felt that reading on the bandstand interfered with sponteneity. So there were no arrangements. "Dannie Richmond had to sing them to me." For Dannie, playing Mingus music had become, in his words, "butter off a duck." On the downbeat, Dannie said, "Don't worry, man." Now Mingus was bellowing at Johnson, "Pedal tones! Play pedal tones!"

Ordinarily Johnson played pedal tones quite comfortably. He had fooled around with them a lot.

Here the key kept changing every four bars. One pedal didn't work.

While Johnson was dutifully "attempting to find a universal pedal," Mingus threw his bass down and came rushing toward the piano. "I thought the end had come. He jammed his face up close to mine. That was the awesome part, when we were nose to nose. Then he took his two gigantic fists and started to bang on the bass end of the piano. I was mortified."

Johnson's humiliation slowly turned to indignation. By the middle of the next solo, he was furious: He was pounding the bass end of the piano with *his* fists. Mingus was impressed with Johnson's nerve. "That hit, that hit!" he hollered out, and then, turning to the audience, declared, "That white boy can really play that thing."

Mingus never lied on stage. As actors say, he was always "in the moment." Audiences loved him for insisting that they share his process, even on the nights he turned on them, lecturing and screaming on how they ought to listen.

He would also wear costumes, a new one sometimes every night. There were big black sombreros, African regalia, Chinese motifs. One night he showed up on the bandstand of the Village Gate in priest's robes. He was the Marlon Brando *and* the Laurence Olivier of jazz.

Whenever he applied his showmanship to explosions off the stage—the threatening letters to editors, fracases with cab drivers and landlords and cops—Mingus was in trouble, hand-cuffed, fired or evicted, or taken to The Tombs.

No question that his temper changed his fate. As a young man, one critical rampage had resulted in his departure from his dream job—as bass player in Duke Ellington's band. After some backstage racial set-to, Juan Tizol, the trombonist and arranger, came at Mingus on the bandstand with a bolo knife. Mingus countered, chasing Tizol with a fire ax. Tizol had seniority (he came at everyone with a bolo knife), and Ellington, who didn't fire anybody, asked Mingus to resign. Ellington, whom Mingus admired deeply, had a more Apollonian temperament, or, as Mingus said once to me wistfully, "He wanted a pleasant band."

The priest who was present at Duke Ellington's deathbed conveyed the Duke's perspicuous final reflection on Mingus. Charles Mingus, his idol said, was "somethin' else."

Mingus claimed that his reputation "forced" him into being a bandleader, that "I got such a bad name, no one would hire me," that he "enjoyed playing other people's music," that he would have been "much happier writin' the music for someone else's band." But even after he had acquired his own fancy honorary college degrees, his American Express card and his taste for rare champagne, it was hard to imagine Mingus at the Rainbow Room playing "A-Train."

❖   ❖   ❖

AL YOUNG USED TO DISTINGUISH between Mingus "shenanigans" and Mingus music. (The press referred to Mingus as "the Angry Man of Jazz.") Frankly, I could never see the difference. It always puzzled me that people took his outbursts so literally, with so much fear.

For example, Mingus took outspoken, impassioned political positions. Yet political commentary resulted in his most mocking, satirical music. He was the composer of "Fables of Faubus," "Oh, Lord, Don't Let Them Drop That Atomic Bomb on Me," "Remember Rockefeller at Attica," "Freedom," "Free Cell Block F, 'Tis Nazi USA." Inevitably he found a musical way to express his feelings. If he couldn't find a musical way, he would let them out any way. But usually he operated with a subtext, metaphorically. You had to read him that way or mistake his anger for violence, his spirituality for madness, his fears for negritude and his cosmic conjurings for paranoia.

For instance, Mingus often threatened that he should have been a pimp. Billy Bones, a pimp whom he invokes as a great sage from time to time in *Beneath the Underdog*, was more than just a dear acquaintance: Billy Bones was a symbol for him of a road not taken, of easy money and camaraderie and street approval and flash that a young man from a ghetto gives up when he commits himself to being, as Mingus was, relentlessly, an artist.

Mingus was a giant, with larger than life qualities (he once had a chess set with rooks as big as beer cans). You had to see how difficult it was for him to cram himself into the confines of black *or* white American society. It was like putting a circus into a bathtub.

During his full-dress Pimp Period, I think in early 1964, Mingus offered to "turn me out." He said, "I'll show you how to be a whore." At the time it seemed flattering. I worked at the *New York Review of Books* for eighty-five dollars a week. My predecessor married Arthur Schlesinger, Jr. I was ready to become a whore. Mingus said I'd be a good one. He wore a diamond stickpin and spoke with some authority. He made it seem like fun. I put on high heels for the next step, an introduction to Trude Heller, the imposing proprietress of a frightening tourist nightclub on Sixth Avenue with a neon sign that bore her name. Over the din, Trude Heller seemed pleased to see Mingus, if not fascinated that I was learning how to be a whore. Trude Heller was busy. It was 11:30 P.M., right before the second show. She sat us at the good end of the bar and bought us each a drink. The band and the singer wore orange satin ruffles and played bar mitzvah arrangements of popular tunes. After only two numbers, Mingus said he was hungry for "Chinese snails," the small ones, with black bean sauce. Some pimp.

For all the bravado, Mingus was deep and open in his feelings about women, more than enough, compared to other men. After four failed marriages, he had utopian views about true love, the perfect integration of the yin and yang. To me they seemed old-fashioned, macho, idealistic and reassuring.

In a back booth at the Ninth Circle, Mingus is not so happy that Lenny Bruce is saying "cunt" so much in front of me. Mingus is glowering from the doorway of a Village party, making sure nothing enjoyable happens to me or Snooky Nazarro, the star bartender of the Ninth Circle, of all times. In bar terminology, Snooky has an "old lady." And a barful of young ladies. There are smoky seminars with Frank Mabry, the race car driver. Mingus wants me to hear his opinions *vis-à-vis* the "asshole in Rhode Island." He says Frank Mabry is "mean." He dismisses a black suitor as "not socially good enough." He thinks this hardship on a Jewish girl and not a princess may be too extreme.

Mingus was an ESP man, a bandleader, orchestrative. *All* the time.

"Oh, yeah," Al Young agrees. "He was a big busybody."

❖ ❖ ❖

THE YEAR OF HIS GREAT TRIUMPH at the Monterey Jazz Festival, 1964, Mingus met Susan Graham—Sue—and they were a mythic couple, in my opinion, together for fifteen years, married (by Allen Ginsberg and then New York State) in 1975. Susan Graham Ungaro Mingus is a startlingly blonde and beautiful woman, with a mind like a lawnmower and the cheekbones of an Indian. She interpreted and managed Mingus's career, daily dealt with jazz musicians, kept jazz musicians' hours. She schlepped around all night at nightclubs. She got up each morning to write journals of this nightlife and to edit and publish *Changes*, a distinguished New York monthly on the counterculture and the arts. After her graduation from Smith College, she had gone to Paris to work on the *Herald-Tribune*. She met and married her first husband, Alberto Ungaro, a sculptor, in Rome. She spoke fluent, fast Italian with a flat Milwaukee accent. She used jazz musicians' jargon with the same integrity. She cooked fabulous and lavish dinners. She had been living alone with Susanna and Roberto, then small children, when Charles Mingus came into their lives.

Susan Graham's connection to Mingus was so strong, and her acceptance of him so deep, that she seemed almost naive about the extravagances of his personality. "Charles never does anything in a small way," she once explained. "If he has one bike, he will have three or four bikes. If he has one camera, he'll have five. He goes into a store to buy a pencil, he'll buy ten boxes of pencils. He went into a store once to buy a knife and bought the whole rack."

Their relationship survived many tempestuous episodes. Once, for some imagined and Othelloesque betrayal, Mingus pulled a knife on Sue. It was a penknife. He backed her into a corner, and when he seemed to have her trapped he said, "What was the name of that guy who stabbed his wife?"

"What?" Sue said.

"He'd understand what I'm trying to do, Sue," said Mingus.

"What do you mean, Charles?" Sue asked, eyes on the penknife.

"The guy who stabbed his wife, Sue. You know what I mean. The writer. It was in the paper. Years ago."

"You mean Norman Mailer?" she said.

"Yeah, that's the one," said Mingus. "The one who sat in the back one time when I was playing at the Half Note."

❖   ❖   ❖

WHEN ANN MCINTOSH FINISHED graduate philosophy studies in Ann Arbor, she picked the New York theater as the place to be a secretary. Under the auspices of her "boss," a woman, Lyn Austin, a Broadway producer, we started an experimental theater, the Loft, on Bleecker Street above the Cafe Go-Go, where Lenny Bruce was busted. The Loft began as a playwrights' theater, since we knew mainly writers. We wanted our theater to be jazzy, and plays seemed rigid, ordinary. Through no deliberate or conscious influence of Mingus, we became involved in improvisational theater, an art form developed in the late fifties by white bohemian intellectuals like Elaine May at the University of Chicago, with aesthetic ambitions, libertarian politics and marketing problems similar to those of jazz. I was like an addict. I gave up everything to improvise, including my prized ninety-five dollars a week job at the *New York Review of Books*, and all the free books. I started an improvisational company, Group Banana, and was doing every which thing as an actor or writer to maintain my swell style of life.

After a rehearsal, I am at Max's Kansas City with a fellow improviser, David Dozer, the man I soon would team up with and live with, and not so soon would marry. Not without alarm I notice Mingus, all too ready to give a new boyfriend the business.

Wisely, David hides his admiration for Mingus, his idol since high school. A poker player, he keeps a poker face. In the freezing cold both king-sized men compete to hail a Checker cab. We trudge up the five flights to my apartment, now on Jones Street, where we juice on and Mingus demonstrates how a jazz great can stuff his Lloyd's of London fingers in an electrical socket without electrocution. Bird or Miles, he says, could also do it. David doesn't flinch. The fingers move out of the socket and toward their drink. If there were townspeople, they would now rejoice. If there were coffee, El Exegente has approved the beans.

❖   ❖   ❖

AT A SPRAWLING ESTATE IN MILLBROOK, New York, in 1967, we are movie actors in a psychedelic Western scenario David has written, *Indiangivers*, one that will be shot here (in every sense of the word) throughout this golden summer of hippie history. David in clown white is playing Dracula. Mingus is playing Pancho Villa bald. Famous hippies like Ultra Violet and Wavy Gravy play in other parts. Horses have been painted green. A Dalmatian, Spot, is violent pink. I am spray-painted silver for my role as Joan of Arc.

This Bavarian gingerbread-style mansion is the headquarters for Dr. Timothy Leary's League for Spiritual Discovery, a religion named so its acronym will correspond with the hallucinogen that is its sacrament. Mingus has been here many times. He was introduced to Leary by the Hitchcocks, who have loaned their country property to the cause. Mingus is not involved with LSD as a tool of salvation, and so far as I know has never even taken it. But he is impressed by Leary's operation here, and I think also with his professorship. He knows a jazz musician would not receive a salary and a mansion to experiment with getting high.

The psychedelic movement has in fact become a nonprofit religious corporation, and the drug-taking is not so pure. There are other trips than LSD here.

Marijuana, hash, STP, DMT, are also approved love-drugs. If you share it, so is gin. I am sitting disconsolately in flaked-out company in the mansion library, remembering that Aldous Huxley believed that LSD could open "the doors of perception." Everyone here is in a stupor. Through French doors I see a hippie carrying four buckets of paint. Soon he is coloring in the leaves and the animals on the dining room tapestries. Mingus enters the library. He is semi- retired from music, has not recorded since 1965, and will not for three more years. He is carrying some music and is swathed in a white toga, his rehearsal clothes, a sheet. I await the camera in my suit of mail.

Reluctantly has Mingus agreed to be cast as a warrior. At home in his studio on the Lower East Side, he maintains an arsenal of self-protective weapons. Here, he worries if it is appropriate for a black man to be draped like this, with bullets, to carry guns onscreen. Once in costume, before the camera, he reacts differently. After "cut" is called, Mingus is still into it, shooting away.

Timothy Leary has arrived on the location from some legal business out of town. He is having some problems with the script. The director calls a meeting in Leary's quarters in the mansion. He and his teenaged daughter Susan share a private wing.

At Leary's kitchen table, joined by Severn Darden, the great improvising actor, we watch Leary cook fried chicken, at the same time as he expounds on art. He wants to throw away the scenario, and his part (the Stagecoach Driver Who Takes Passengers on Trips), and wing it, sort of let the cameras roll. As the high priest of ego loss, his is the ego of the hour, and he will eventually have his way. The footage will be abandoned by the producer to a vault in Movie Lab, and shooting will resume at Millbrook with a new scenario, *The Story of Timothy Leary*, after the director has allegedly distracted himself with a glass of LSD.

Now, Leary, turning over chicken, says he has a friend, a real Apache. The movie he would make this second is the story of the real Apache, because he wouldn't even need to act.

Timothy Leary was, and seems to remain, a bullshit artist, a flyweight, a presumptuous man.

Mingus listens for a long time to Dr. Leary's anarchic approach to spontaneous art, Mingus's art, improvisation. "You can't improvise on nothin', man," Mingus says at last. "You gotta improvise on somethin'."

❖   ❖   ❖

THROUGH THESE TIPSY TIMES, Mingus is in his Bicycle Period, pedaling through the Village on a folding bike practicing Flower Power. I am returning from Bohack's supermarket when he pulls up at the curb with daffodils. Then he hits the trail. I watch him waft off into traffic like a Macy's parade balloon, waving angelically.

❖   ❖   ❖

THERE WAS A RHYTHM TO THE MAN as spontaneous and hard to notate as jazz. His talk was filled with offbeat punctuations, catcalls, hollers. Some words he bent, some words he chirped. He excelled at African sounding gibberish, and could do a creditable old school tie accent. Some words he seemed to have invented. Whitney Balliett observed that "Mingus talks in leaping slurs . . . sometimes the words move so fast whole sentences are unintelligible. It is an obstacle he is well aware of." If he wanted to mumble, he would mumble. Sometimes he would sullenly refuse to talk at all. He had a whole network and lexicon of private images, nicknames, code words. He dated things by his ex-wives.

For an approximation of this vocal phenomenon, try reciting very fast the title of this Mingus tune: "All the Things You Could Be by Now If Sigmund Freud's Wife Was Your Mother." Allow the natural stress to occur at the word "be" and slow down to a glide on the word "mother." That is Mingus talking. Now say it over slowly. That is Mingus thinking.

Charles Mingus III, the playwright and painter, Mingus's oldest son, once told me over a breakfast of radishes and vodka that his father's mental speed exceeded the speed at which his thoughts could be articulated. "He can say things you don't ever hear," Mingus III explained. "The way to understand him is . . . sensing by tone with certain key indicators." In other words, it was not an easy thing to be his son.

In fact, Mingus believed the voice to be an improvisational instrument, and the effect of his method was to force you to listen to him. If you did, as one musician noted after Mingus had taught him how to play a tune, "he can show you the processes of his mind." "He's not talking about day to day, simple stuff," said Mingus III. "Sometimes I think I have to spend twenty years in a Jesuit seminary to decipher what he's aimin' at."

I remember a promotional party for a group that Benny Golson and Art Farmer formed in 1962 called the Jazztet. Frank Mabry, the race car driver, drove us to it in his hand-tooled leather pimpmobile. The party was in the East Side apartment of a white photographer and his wife. The house was Bauhaus-pure, all chrome and leather. They were wheeling away a tea cart of Chinese take-out foods when we came in, in time for the dessert: pineapple chunks stuck with toothpicks. Benny Golson and Art Farmer, the guests of honor, were there, dignified in ties and tiny-checkered suits. All the black people were dressed nicely and with great restraint, to accommodate the leather and the chrome. Among them, Mingus stood out like the surprise at the stag party, dressed in a sweatsuit, a gray one, woolly socks and sneakers and a ski cap, bright blue. I had added my voice to the polite hum of conversation and was spearing a pineapple chunk when I heard Mingus launch into a tirade, a real cascade of leaping slurs. We never heard the details, but the essence lingered on: "Charlie Parker wouldn't have wanted us to end up this way." Benny Golson and Art Farmer seemed much more amused than the photographer's wife.

I reminded Mingus of that incident a long time later. I wanted to know how Charlie Parker wanted them to wind up. He didn't remember the tirade, but he did remember the pineapple chunks. "They didn't know how to eat," he explained.

Mingus did. Once, over Mingus's protests that a man his size be seated at a larger table, a waiter insisted on seating him and Susan Graham at a table for two. Mingus ordered four steak dinners. To serve them, the waiter had to carry in a second table.

When she was a teenager, he told Sue's daughter, Susanna, that he was in the mood for her specialty, spaghetti and meatballs. Susanna was flattered. She cooked up a big pot. Mingus ate it all. "How was it, Charles?" asked the chef. "Wasn't spicy enough," he said.

For Mingus's *New Yorker* profile, Whitney Balliett moved along with him from one restaurant to another. Mingus followed a dinner of Pouilly-Fuisse and lobster tails with a snack of champagne and clams. These meals had been preceded by the Ninth Circle's cheese platter and a Ramos gin fizz. Ramos Gin Fizz requires such ingredients as an egg white and orange flower water, besides the gin. Bartenders are often reluctant to make them. Usually, Mingus told Balliett, he ordered ten.

Mingus was a good cook too, with a fearless hand. I remember being driven downtown to the Village from a dinner at Mingus and Judy's apartment—no longer in Harlem, but on Upper Fifth Avenue. Mingus called it "Jackie Kennedy's neighborhood." Beside me in the taxi was Edmund White, the writer, another college friend. When we hit midtown, Ed White also thought the lights were ricocheting off the Plaza fountain like fireworks. We were seeing stars from the Chateau Lafite-Rothschild and brandy sauce on Mingus's rabbit stew.

Mingus's holiday eggnog was a concoction so delicious and mind-blowing, you would do anything to make sure that you saw him at Christmas. Over the phone once, he gave me the recipe:

- Separate one egg for one person. Each person gets an egg.
- Two sugars for each egg, each person.
- One shot of rum, one shot of brandy per person.
- Put all the yolks into one big pan, with some milk.
- That's where the 151 proof rum goes. Put it in gradually or it'll burn the eggs.

- ✦ OK. The whites are separate and the cream is separate.
- ✦ In another pot—depending on how many people—put in one shot of each, rum and brandy. (This is after you whip your whites and your cream.)
- ✦ Pour it over the top of the milk and yolks.
- ✦ One teaspoon of sugar. Brandy and rum.
- ✦ Actually you mix it all together.
- ✦ Yes, a lot of nutmeg. Fresh nutmeg. And stir it up.
- ✦ You don't need ice cream unless you've got people coming and you need to keep it cold. Vanilla ice cream. You can use eggnog. I use vanilla ice cream.
- ✦ Right, taste for flavor. Bourbon? I use Jamaica Rum in there. Jamaican *Rums*. Or I'll put rye in it. Scotch. It depends. See, it depends on how drunk I get while I'm tasting it.

✦　　✦　　✦

THIS WINTER OF 1971, the Black Panthers are throwing a fund-raising party for themselves in Brooklyn, right across the bridge. Sue wants us to go, Mingus is unenthusiastic. Politically, he is a solitary cat. We enter a gutted factory building by way of a makeshift schoolroom, the place to leave the coats. Childishly lettered "Black is beautiful" drawings line the walls. A few young black men are milling here, acting supervisory. They solemnly direct us to a room beyond: smoky, blaring, jammed. Strobe lights blink across a vast distance, possibly the size of a basketball court. Hundreds of people are dancing to an electronically-loud band. A soul kitchen, surrounded by yards of squared-off serving tables, is manned remarkably by four or five young Aunt Jemimas. They are hoisting tubs of greens and potato salad and shouting sass to the crowds that keep forming for the next batch of fried chicken. A platter costs $1.50. The beverge of the night is Afro-Cola, which boldly features a turbaned black profile on the can. Fine print reveals that Pepsico distributes it. The chicken line is very long. "Hey, Sue," comments Mingus, "Where's that place where I ate lobsters?" He means he thinks we'd better split.

We return to the schoolroom for our coats. It is crowded now with Panthers and Panther families mingling with musicians unpacking instruments, waiting to perform. As Mingus enters, the crowd parts, forming an invisible red carpet for him. Coolly, Mingus returns respectful hand slaps and makes his royal exit.

❖   ❖   ❖

MINGUS IS FOCUSED ON MUSIC AGAIN. His supposedly fallow Bicycle and Photography periods of the late sixties have resulted in a new album, *Let My Children Hear Music*, containing a "Special Bonus Enclosure: Provocative Essay by Charles Mingus," a thoughtful and sophisticated diagnosis of the problems of a "spontaneous composer" with the economics of jazz. David and I run into him on Broadway and Fiftieth, two blocks from the old Birdland, at the Woolworth's popcorn stand.

In order to work with his equals in these rock and roll years, he will be organizing a number of important concerts of "Charles Mingus and Friends," which shall combine the musical energies of both his peers and his proteges under Mingus's unusually relaxed, almost indulgent hand. Mingus has surprisingly little ego about his own performance. He is turned off by show-offs, "guys who dance around with their instruments." In the face of a lot of applause, he seems shy. Playing with masters like Gene Ammons and Dizzy Gillespie, he is choosing the role of the host, not the star.

After the great 1972 concert at Philharmonic Hall, a group of family and friends accompany Mingus to dinner at the Ninth Circle. The dinner orders are arriving at the table. The group, hungry and cutthroat, is nit-picking the concert: Bill Cosby, the co-producer and guest emcee, had turned a dignified event into a Las Vegas lounge act, overdoing it with too much shtick; with so generous an audience, the sidemen played interminable solos; Dizzy Gillespie hogged the stage. Finally, we turn to Mingus for his own report of "Charles Mingus and Friends." Mingus looks up from his plate. "Too many friends," he says.

❖   ❖   ❖

ROLLING STONE ONCE ASKED ME to write about Mingus, interesting to them as a precursor of the more commercial "fusion" jazz. In the seventies, fashionable groups had even taken to recording fifties Mingus tunes. Listening to one rendition of "Goodbye Porkpie Hat," Susan Graham asked Mingus, "What does that sound like to you?" "Money," he replied.

It was the first time in our relationship that I had ever played the part of "the press." And the last thing I was interested in was asking him anything that wasn't oblique, cut on the bias. In music his own approach to rhythm was: "You draw a picture away from the beat right up to its core with different notes of different sounds of the drum instruments so continuously that the core is always there for an open mind . . . if one tries to stay inside dead center or directly on top of the beat or on the bottom, the beat is too rigid on the outside where it is heard." And I had seen too many fans and jazz buffs go down in defeat, pissing him off with musical opinions he regarded as moronic. About his music, Mingus could be very snooty.

Once he wanted to do a nightclub act with David, after he saw him improvise. The act would consist of spontaneous dialogues that illuminated the difference between blacks and whites. In a controversy, for instance, about the moon, David, the white man, would take the rational, scientific side of the fight. ("The moon is a satellite which revolves around the earth monthly at a mean distance of 238,857 miles.") Mingus, the black man, would be playful and poetic. ("The moon is a green little man made of cheese.")

David was enthusiastic about the act, but it was summer, and in short-sleeved shirts their complexions were identical, both taffy-colored. The act needed more elements of conflict. "I play the drums, Charles," David said. "I learned in high school. When you want to get mad at the white guy, I can play the drums while you play the bass." "You play drums with me?" Mingus shot back. "What jazz poll'd you ever win?"

I didn't usually get into that. Once Mingus and I had a brief exchange about my singing lessons, a subject I felt reasonably competent to discuss. "Listen to Billie Holiday," was his advice. "She just follows the pitch and talks the song. You already can do that." I said I wanted to sing like Carmen McRae. He beamed with approval. "You been listenin'," he said.

At the time of our interview, August 1974, Mingus was deeply immersed in his Cigar Period, which had begun that spring on a vacation in the free port of St. Maarten. "I was smokin' cheap cigars. I was

Janet
Coleman

smokin' Grenadiers. J.C. Suares turned me on to good cigars. I didn't smoke as often as I do now that I've got good cigars." He had naturally invested in a splendid humidor and was already experimenting with connoisseur improvements on the flavor of cigars. One trick had to do with apple peels, another involved damp toilet paper.

In Montreal between engagements of a major concert tour, he had bought five boxes of Havanas. In New York he was planning to pack the empty boxes, so he could refill them with more Havanas at the next and presumably each subsequent duty-free store.

His layover is two nights only. Mingus wants to spend them at Bradley's, the jazz bar on University Place. He wants the owner, Bradley, to have a good cigar. I meet him and Susan Graham there. One glance and I can tell that it is not his night. Already his wine is corked, his steak wrapped in a doggie bag. Two boxes of cigars are stacked on the table. I turn on the tape recorder and hope for the best. I feel I have a job to do.

"And how was Canada?"

"All right, Canada," he says. "Much as any place else. All I saw was the hotel and the job."

"You admire Eddie Gomez. Why is he so great?"

"He plays a more complicated instrument. Bass players know it."

"Why do the polls usually pick Ray Brown as best bassist?"

"I don't know."

"You did last week."

Now on the bandstand at Bradley's, Bob Dorough has finished singing "Yardbird Suite," and his fine rendition at the piano of "I Get the Neck of the Chicken" is rolling onto my tape.

"Who do you like better, John Lennon or Mick Jagger?" I go on.

"I don't know either of their work," he replies.

"Come again?" I say. I've heard his grudging comments on the Beatles.

"I saw his name on the jukebox," he concedes. "John Lennon. In Canada."

I order a double rum.

"A Chinese jukebox," he says.

"You went to a Chinese restaurant in Canada?" I ask.

"They all sound alike to me," says Mingus. "Like little marching men."

"Rock and roll musicians, you mean?" Mingus nods slightly. Yes.

"What did Charlie Parker eat?"

"Eat? Everything. As far as I know."

"Did he eat a lot?"

"I don't know. Never seen him eat."

"You never saw Charlie Parker eat? How come?"

"Never had dinner together."

"You never did?" I say quite loud, combining real and feigned surprises.

"Lunch or breakfast."

"I'm surprised to hear that. Do you think anybody _____ 47

ever did?" I stick with it, wagging my hands. "No one ever talks about it, you know. It's not part of the legend."

I am looking at Mingus from the corner of my eye. His head is bent down on his chest. His eyes are focused on his buttons, listening.

"If he was mystical and had so many things that he did," I conclude, "he would probably have things that he ate."

His head comes up. "I never even saw him eat a sandwich." He takes a deep breath. "Max said he saw him eat out of a bag one time."

"What?"

"Max Roach said he saw him eatin' out of a bag one time. I don't know what it was. Somethin' in a bag."

I slap the tape recorder in triumph. Mingus calls the waitress and orders a double Fine Anejo, a Coca-Cola chaser and a side of lime.

"So what is jazz?"

"Nigger music."

"Why do you always play 'I Can't Get Started'?"

"'Cause I can't get started."

Then Mingus gathers up the steak and wine, finds Bradley and delivers the cigar.

He exits in the wrong direction, toward the Cedar Bar, where Mingus tells the bartender how he smuggled the boxes of cigars across the border in the inside pockets of his trenchcoat. He trades the bartender two drinks for two cigars.

"It's very weird," he says to me, when this transaction is completed. "I never even saw him eat a hot dog. He must've got hungry sometime." He is squinting toward the jukebox as it plays Marvin Hamlisch's bestselling arrangement of Scott Joplin's rags.

"He never ate out," he says to me. "He'd eat at home, that's probably why."

"He had a home?" I ask.

"With Chan. All the time I knew him he was with Chan."

"So she knew the secret."

"Whether he ate or not. Yeah."

On the street, Sue and Mingus wait with me to get a cab.

"I wonder if anyone knows what Shakespeare ate," Sue says.

"I never saw him eat an apple. Or even chew a stick of gum," Mingus says. "He only played."

❖   ❖   ❖

CHANGES PARTY, CHRISTMAS 1974. There is no eggnog at the Mingus house this year. Mingus has been incarcerated for much of the winter, dieting at a health farm near Woodstock. He has lost forty pounds eating vegetables and has decided eggs are unhealthful. There is glog instead. Vats of it. A turkey. Cheeses. Hams.

The party is an ode to beatnik history. Among the guests are Allen Ginsberg, Peter Orlovsky, Gregory

Corso. So are the jazz entrepreneurs, Art D'Lugoff and Max Gordon, whose club, the Village Vanguard, will feature Mingus as soon as he decides he's thin enough to leave the health farm. In the kitchen, Gordon, a tiny man, confides that he can't notice a forty-pound difference in Mingus. Mingus looks exactly the same to him. And then thinking that he must be drunk, Gordon, in a courtly fashion, rubs his head and leaves the party.

Propped on the kitchen table near a piece of wet cheesecloth containing fruit peelings and used spices from the glog is a certificate from a European jazz society naming Charles Mingus Composer of the Year. That personage is sitting on a church pew in the living room, benignly eating the lemon peels out of his glog. I am very touched by this gathering of the best minds of a generation.

"Hey, Allen," Mingus calls, and Ginsberg leans in eagerly to hear him. "How come you guys only like to fuck in the asshole?" Allen Ginsberg does a double take, and then his face breaks into a beatific smile.

"We *don't* only like to fuck in the asshole, Charlie," he explains. "Peter and I like to fuck each other in the asshole, in the armpit, and the elbow . . . behind the knees."

Mingus nods with understanding. "I fucked someone in the asshole once," he says to Ginsberg. "By mistake."

A large group of us go for an after-party drink to Bradley's. Mingus is welcomed and back-patted back from the health farm by the Bradley regulars. He acknowledges the greeting by ordering a magnum of vintage champagne. Already reeling from glog, I am startled to see Thelonious Monk walk by our table. There is no greeting between Monk and Mingus, just a reverberation, like two ocean liners passing in the night. Monk enters the men's room, and Mingus pours champagne. "Hey, Monk," says Mingus when Monk sails out again. "Whyn't you come visit me at the health farm? Good for your health on a farm."

Without disturbing a beat of his rhythm, Monk smiles and mutters and doffs his hat. I have no idea what he has muttered, whether he has answered yes or no to the visit. But Mingus seems buoyed by this encounter. When the waitress is called for the second magnum of champagne, Mingus asks for a big dish of ice cream too, he doesn't care what flavor.

❖   ❖   ❖

I READ PARTS OF MY MEMOIR to Mingus during the raw vegetable dinner he requests on my sixth wedding anniversary, in February 1975. Mingus likes it. "That's better than the stuff about me in *down beat*, Sue," he says. "That stuff ain't shit."

Next the four of us, in Village clothes, are at the St. Regis Maisonette to hear Sarah Vaughan. Mingus has sent her the music and his own purple lyrics to a new composition, "Duke Ellington's Sound of Love," a tribute, a gorgeous song. Susan Graham once observed that "Charles would have made a great A&R man." Sarah Vaughan is an inspired choice to introduce the song. She may sing it tonight at this chi-chi nightclub that looks like Adolph Menjou's library. It is almost incumbent upon Mingus to fortify his raw vegetable diet with a 1922 champagne. When a silver tray of complimentary pastries is passed by the waiter, Mingus grumpily takes six. Sarah Vaughan performs a breathtaking set. Before her last number, she shuffles some music she says shyly she is still rehearsing and plunges into a masterpiece in progress, her version of Stephen Sondheim's "Send in the Clowns."

In the lobby of the St. Regis, Mingus is ordering around a series of Sarah Vaughan's supernumeraries and managers on the hotel phone. The tedious politics of the music business grind on. "Hey, Mama," Mingus says at last to Sarah Vaughan. "How come you don't sing my song?"

❖   ❖   ❖

MINGUS, SUMMER 1975, is in the hospital with a slipped disc. When I ask for his room number the receptionist says, "You mean *Charlie?*" He has been fasting five days, and for hospital gifts his only request is "razor blades." In the room is Paul

Jeffry, a jazz disc jockey who works for Yamaha, leafing through the page proofs of Wilfred Sheed's forthcoming book on Muhammed Ali. I ask Mingus why jazz musicians don't endorse each other's records as authors do each other's books. My remark inspires from Paul Jeffry a heated attack on record companies. They don't want jazz records to get ahead. They want to rip off black music. Benny Goodman was *not* the King of Swing. I have heard these arguments before. Why don't the musicians get together, I resume, and endorse each other's records? Mingus, on his back in bed, opens up a pack of Trident gum. "Jazz musicians," he says, "are the most selfish, conceited, self-centered, *greedy* group of people in the world. Some of these young guys I see, they think they're God." Neatly, he stuffs the gum wrapper into a paper cup. In an hour he will phone Susan Graham to locate a chiropractor and a Stilton cheese in the refrigerator and to bring them both with her to the hospital. Tomorrow he will call me early to urge me to the hospital with a box of Kentucky Fried Chicken. Now he chews gum a few seconds and shrugs. "Maybe they are God," he says.

❖　　❖　　❖

IN 1961 HE WROTE TO HIMSELF and sent the words that Judy typed to me:

Perhaps someday the musicians will profit as well as their barterers, barkers, and sacred professional friends that crap up the scene intentionally to confuse the profit where they think best, their pockets; and the few toms who this far have been satisfied with their picture in their magazines and less than fifty percent of their salaries in their pockets . . .

Mingus himself had checked out Satan. "I was a studio musician once, in California. No joke, yeah. They make a lot of money, studio musicians. I know guys won't come *home* without $900 a week. That's the *minimum*. They'd all like to play jazz, but see, they can't."

He knew what he had passed up to be his own musician. "I'd have a house and a home by now." House *and* home! "And a yacht. And a Cadillac like all them other guys got. Cadillac and a yacht. And a house with wheels on it . . ."

❖   ❖   ❖

THE MINGUS BAND HAS DRIVEN down from Newport to Lenox, Massachusetts, in 1971 for a July Fourth concert Ann McIntosh is producing in the courtyard amphitheater of the Music Inn. The courtyard is surrounded by a mall of small boutiques. The Thembi Arts Center, the African boutique, has mailed Min-

gus an invitation to its holiday photo display of Eric
Dolphy. The four brothers in attendance, Kunle
Mwanga and three assistants, lead the way to the
snapshots. Mingus nods at them abstractedly. He is
more interested in a huge white caftan, trimmed
with gold embroidery. It is a perfect fit.

The Red Lion Inn, famous in these parts since the
American Revolution, a bastion of courteous, re-
strained New England, is serving lunch today. From
a meal twenty years earlier, Mingus remembers how
to get there. Trailed by an entourage of Susan
Graham, David and me, Mingus, in the African robe
he refers to as "my dress," crosses Route 7, where
Norman Rockwell lives, a perfect cover for the Sat-
urday Evening Post.

In June 1977, Mingus is on the front lawn of the
White House, confined to a wheelchair, receiving
honors from the President. Mingus responds to the
crowd's ovation by bursting into tears. Jimmy Carter runs to hug him. Under the circumstances, the
news media reports these unashamed emotions
with respect.

Approaching the peak of his worldly powers, in
November 1977, Mingus's illness was diagnosed as
amyotrophic lateral sclerosis, "Lou Gehrig's Disease," a disorder of the muscle and the nervous sys-
tems with no known cause or cure. He had inflicted
murderous assaults on his own body. This was not
one of them. It was an unspeakably cruel fate.

Susan Graham was told he had three months to

live. He was more and more immobilized, but he lived another year. As a diversion, a mutual friend, Daniel Senatore, introduced Mingus to the work of Joni Mitchell, a white woman and a commercial superstar whose complicated lyrics seemed to suit her new embrace of jazz. They met and liked each other, and under his undiminished spell she wrote lyrics for three of Mingus's tunes. Of their collaboration, Joni Mitchell wrote, "It was as if I had been standing by a river—and Charlie came by and pushed me in—'sink or swim'—him laughing at me dog-paddling around the currents of black classical music."

Without expecting to make the Olympics, Joni Mitchell spent 1978 working hard as Mingus's final protege.

In January 1978, Mingus made his last, a dream recording for Atlantic, *Me, Myself an Eye*, a symphonic production with a twenty-four-piece band. On the final record, Eddie Gomez played the bass.

During this session, Sy Johnson took a photo of a majestic Mingus: He is sitting in a wheelchair, controlling the control booth, beside the saxophones, in a neck brace and a Stetson hat. He is totally concentrated on the music. His fingers are blurry, strumming an imaginary bass.

I was in Los Angeles in 1978, facing my own music. Several times I missed connecting with Sue and Mingus in person in New York. In the fall of the year, they were in seclusion deep in Mexico with a local healer, accepting her cure. I was very frightened. I was positive it would occur. Via Roberto Ungaro I sent a message through to Mexico. Susan Graham reached me before Christmas in New York. Their lease was up and Mingus wanted to move to Los Angeles, a more familiar and efficient place than Mexico, with sun. She asked me to find them a house.

I was a newcomer, an exile in the city. I had only one friend in Los Angeles from Los Angeles, the photographer, Pat Shamroy Shaw. In December she was earning Christmas shopping money as Patty Shamroy by selling real estate. From her mother, Patty Shamroy knew about the house of a jazz record producer, recently deceased. She showed it to Daniel Senatore, the connection to Mexico, and he rented it.

After her divorce from Patty's father, Audrey Shamroy had a child by John Simmons, a black jazz musician who would die the following year at sixty-one. He was one of Mingus's older cousins, through the complex genealogy of Watts. John Simmons had played with Teddy Wilson, Benny Goodman, Errol Garner. He was asked to resign from the band of Duke Ellington. He also played the bass.

Audrey Shamroy first heard her husband's cousin Mingus when he was playing at a club on La Cienega, in from Watts, a young and green musician. Mingus courted one of Audrey Shamroy's girl-friends, but he was more vivid in her memory as "a man alone with his bass."

"Just being alive seems to sometimes place innocent victims and their *tiny* ideas of the gathered truths of the ages in a cocoon of inescapable flesh,"

Mingus wrote me in the spring of 1961. He said then that he "faltered at escape. For too long escape has been a dreaded adventure . . . as I have told you, my hesitation is not one in fear of the darkness of the journey that is *ahead*, but instead is of the *light* on the seeming inobvious subjects of man and God in this Western world."

Before Daniel Senatore called to cancel the rental, Audrey Shamroy already knew from Benny Carter, the saxophone and trumpet player, that Mingus was dead. "The musicians have the fastest line," Audrey Shamroy said.

Mingus died in Cuernevaca on January fifth at the age of fifty-six. In a Mexican paper, Susan Graham noticed this item: The day Mingus's body was cremated, fifty-six whales were discovered beached in Mexico along the shore and burned.

I was in New York when she departed for India to release Mingus's ashes in the Ganges River and to set his spirit free.

Back in Los Angeles the answering service had a message: "Happy New Year. Sue and Charles."

❖   ❖   ❖

THE SUN IS SETTING OVER THE HOLLYWOOD BOWL on the second night of the Playboy Jazz Festival, 1979, and Mingus music is rolling across this vast amphitheater like thunder balls. A phosphorescent neon mission cross is gleaming in the distance behind the band shell in the Hollywood Hills. When Duke Ellington died, Mingus lamented the musical fate of "Duke's dead band." But Mingus's Jazz Workshops were always more unorthodox, experimental pieces of machinery. Mingus Dynasty is a new musical entity featuring an all-star cast of members of former Mingus bands, getting it on under a collective leadership and playing hard, if not their asses off. There have been other adjustments: Dannie Richmond, in his new speaking role as emcee, seems to enjoy showing the flowery side of himself to the public. Susan Graham is pacing on the stage. I have never seen her there before. Did she put on his knowledge with his power? When Mingus Dynasty appeared the week before in San Francisco, Al Young reports that in a rare display of fire, Sue seized the microphone to excoriate the nightclub owner for providing a substandard piano and cheating the band out of bread.

Within a few years, Dandy Dannie also will be prematurely dead. But Susan Graham will persist. And Mingus Dynasty will someday soar, under the leadership of the trombonist Jimmy Knepper (not withstanding the fact that Mingus once punched out his teeth). Not yet.

It is dark when Joni Mitchell introduces her eerie, first-person lyrics about reincarnation to Mingus's final tunes. Blowsy fragments hit the nerve between tragedy and laughter:

MINGUS
MINGUS

In daydreams of rebirth
I see myself in style
Raking in what I'm worth
Next time
I'll be bigger!
I'll be better than ever!
I'll be resurrected royal!
I'll be rich as standard oil!
But now—Manhattan holds me
To a chair in the sky
With the bird in my ears
And boats in my eyes
Going by.

Joni Mitchell is backed by very good musicians, Wayne Shorter and Herbie Hancock. I have the feeling they are lucky that Mingus himself is so benevolently dead tonight. Compared to Mingus's own renditions of his music, they make Easy Listenin', this band.

Later, in the star position of the evening, Sarah Vaughan and her regal instrument perform "Send in the Clowns," a boat in my eyes, going by.

❖ ❖ ❖

I AM TALKING TO MY OLD FRIEND Ann McIntosh, who is running a seminar at Goddard College, in concepts of video and cable communications that I can't even understand. Tonight there is a Mingus memorial concert in New York, on the Top Floor of the Village Gate. The memory of hearing thunder and sunlight in that room is so strong that it does not sound absurd to me when Ann wants to send a telegram to the Village Gate, so Mingus knows that we were there.

❖   ❖   ❖

"IF CHARLIE COULD SEE ME NOW," says Snooky Nazarro in Los Angeles, behind a bar. We drink to Snooky's, a new jazz club on Pico Boulevard. He has to pay Irving, the Smirnoff distributor, and audition chocolate cakes. Snooky finishes first. "Maybe he can," he says. He picks the biggest chocolate cake.

❖   ❖   ❖

AL YOUNG IS TALKING LONG DISTANCE at his desk in Palo Alto. In twenty-four hours he will finish his new novel, *Ask Me Now*. Everybody so far likes it. He guesses it is good. "Mingus always told me in writing to use my own voice. I think I'm doin' it." Al Young's beautiful voice is almost shouting. "I'm gonna get *rich* this year!"

❖   ❖   ❖

I AM HAVING MY HAIR COIFFED beside the snake aquarium in the salon of Susanna Ungaro, Mingus's stepdaughter, mother of two little boys and a licensed cosmetologist. At seventeen, at his request, she gave Mingus her first haircut. "He trusted me with a scissors," no small compliment. In those days, he would fuss that she was tweezing her eyebrows too thin. "That was what I thought was cool then," Susanna says. "They were like a pencil line." Mingus thought they were unladylike. Thus, after a road trip, his gift to her was a Schiaparelli perfume, "Shocking You." "He said it was worn in Paris by the prostitutes."

Years later she revealed to her mother Mingus's beauty tip. Sue scoffed. "She said Charles made up the thing about the prostitutes." Susanna is snipping dead ends off my perm. She smiles like a Roman painting, enigmatically. "I wish I could get more of that perfume. I still have an empty bottle somewhere."

❖   ❖   ❖

IN A SECOND AVENUE CAFE on a muggy summer night, discussing the censorship of hygiene and germ theory among colonial peoples, Einstein's particle wave theory, the internal struggles of Zimbabwe and how to mix acrylic paint, is Mingus's firstborn son, newly liberated at thirty-five from wearing Roman numerals on his name. He flies loop-deloops over the same metaphysical geography as his father, with MIT-type information, in Jack Armstrong's voice. "There are no new worlds to discover," he is saying. "There are millions of worlds to create." At twenty-one, when he arrived from California at the Music, Art and Health loft with his abstract paintings, his father told him he should learn to paint an apple first. Mingus had three other sons (Eugene, Dorian and Eric) and two daughters (Yanine and Carolyn, or "Keki"). His namesake got the hardest time. I remember Mingus promoting that apple after one of Charles III's abstract designs was selected as a Christmas card for the Museum of Modern Art. "Dad was a liberal. He wanted me to go to Harvard and become, you know, a lawyer," Mingus the Younger sighs.

❖   ❖   ❖

CHRISTMAS 1979. On the phone Mingus's stepson, Roberto (now called Robert) Ungaro, is describing the eggnog they have prepared in New York this year from the recipe herein and Roberto's childhood memory of how to work that pan of yolks. Susan Graham says they were smacking their lips when Roberto said, "Charles is still here. He's here in his music. He's here in his eggnog."

❖   ❖   ❖

SPREAD ON THE DINING ROOM TABLE are 100 stamped entries to the 7-Up Super Two Sweepstakes, addressed in different colors, from two big bowls of felt-tipped pens. "Do I feel his presence?" David asks. He raises an eyebrow and a shot of tequila. "I'm working on my art."

"You know, I don't miss Mingus," David says. "Sometimes I wish I could see him again. But I knew him a long time. I never expected him to live long. From the moment I met him he had his fingers in the socket." David is crying. "He was burning too bright."

❖   ❖   ❖

"WERE YOU THERE? Were you there at the old Five Spot?" Mingus asks.

"The one down the street from the new Five Spot?" Yes, I was there. Once. But the band that played was Monk's.

"We used to have dancers come down. Artists would come and paint. Sketches of people posin' and musicians playin'. I should have waited ten years. Before I got any ideas. I was too soon."

❖   ❖   ❖

I DREDGE UP MEMORIES and fit them into the grid: I met him when I was eighteen. He was black. I am white. He was a musician. He was a genius. He could barely spell. I can spell. We both improvised.

Janet Coleman

I am now older than Mingus was when I met him. On my own I have observed that we repress and fear our feelings although it toxifies our lives. The road to spontaneity and freedom is pretty much uphill. I feel lucky that the same incorrigible and incorruptible spirit that informed me when I was young returns so regularly to haunt me now.

Mingus viewed music as an elixir, an antidote to the poison, a religious calling. In a phone conversation with Mingus, the only word you could be sure of was the last one, "love." I got a lot from him. When I was nineteen, I sent him what? A school paper? A story I was working on? Judy typed up the reply. He said, "I read your writings twice. I liked it. Of course I'm speaking of your soul. Your teacher can have the technical opinions. They're only important because that's his job . . . writing is a means of communication.

"I could dismiss it there, but to further my views of teachers, they're probably so involved with the sciences of styles and centuries that that's what their kicks come from, to see who writes like who when actually it's a whole lot of *schitt.* Just write, if you ever did you probably did it the same way a million years."

As I mostly rested on my million years of laurels, he encouraged even more my most uneven improvised endeavors. He liked my spaghetti commercials too. Whatever I was doing, he made me feel that I was not a fool to be an artist, and if someone with his VSOP tastes liked my stuff, I must be doing something right.

To me Mingus personified artistic integrity. In his vocabulary "selling out" remained a well-weathered and a damning phrase. He thought it more honorable to be a pimp or a prostitute. I was never up to those jobs. But I absorbed some of Mingus's guerrilla strategies for surviving as an improvising performer. I learned some Fifty-second Street smarts. As deeply as he believed in jazz, Mingus believed in the laws of copyright, that everyone in show business is out to censor or to rob you, so whenever possible get paid in cash. Not least I learned the way to smoke a good cigar: "Put your mouth around it. Lick it with your lips. Now suck it in, suck it in, Ja-nett. Roll it around in your mouth. That's it! That's it! Taste it! Taste it like fine wine!" When that lesson was over, Mingus leaned back in his chair, folded his arms over his belly and heaved a sigh of satisfaction. "Women look good when they smoke cigars," he said.

❖   ❖   ❖

I RAN INTO HIM AT THE NINTH CIRCLE one night late, oh, twenty-five years ago. He was dressed in a brown banker's suit and vest, and he was drinking vintage wine. At closing time Mingus offered to escort me home if I waited while he got some things he'd stored in the coatroom. I thought he meant his top hat and cane. When he came out of the coat room he was dressed in a yellow slicker suit with matching hat and boots. He had a bow and quiver on his shoulder and a suitcase in his hand. We walked to Balducci's, then an all-night fruit stand on Greenwich Avenue, and stopped to buy some apples. A street acquaintance passed and asked him what was in the suitcase. Mingus opened it. It was full of extra arrows.

❖   ❖   ❖

Mingus's father, Charles Mingus 1st, age 33.
Photo courtesy Charles Mingus III

Charles "Barron" Mingus, publicity shot, Los Angeles, c. 1947.

Canilla Jean Gross Mingus Page, 1945, Mingus's first wife, Los Angeles, 1945.

Photos courtesy Celia Mingus Zaentz (L) and Charles Mingus III (R)

Mingus and son (Charles Mingus III), California, c. 1945.
Photo courtesy Charles Mingus III

Mingus and Celia Gemanis Mingus atop the Hotel Maryland on their wedding day, New York City, April 2, 1951.

Photo courtesy Celia Mingus Zaentz

Mingus with Spaulding Givens rehearsing first Debut album, *Strings & Keys*, 1952.   Photo courtesy Celia Mingus Zaentz

Charlie Parker and Mingus,
Birdland 1953.
Photo Courtesy Celia Mingus Zaentz

Charlie Parker and Mingus,
Birdland 1953.
Photo Courtesy Celia Mingus Zaentz

(left to right) Charlie Parker, Bud Powell, Mingus; Birdland 1953.
Photo Courtesy Celia Mingus Zaentz

Mingus posed himself at the piano for this publicity
photo, c. 1961. Even then it was important for him to
be viewed as a composer, not just a bass player.

Al Young, college student at University of Michigan, 1960.
Photo by Thayer Burch

Mingus with Janet Coleman and unidentified party guests, Christmas 1964.
Photo courtesy Sue Mingus

Window: Judith Starkey Mingus (R) and Carolyn "Keki" Mingus (L),
New York City, 1964.   Photo courtesy Carolyn "Keki" Mingus

Janet Coleman as Joan of Arc and
Mingus as Pancho Villa, on the
set of *Indiangivers*, Millbrook,
New York, summer 1967.
Photo by Diane Dorr-Dorynek

Mingus making up as Pancho V
for the production of the
Indiangivers, Millbrook, New
York, summer 1967.
Photo by Diane Dorr-Dorynek

(left to right) Timothy Leary, Mingus, Severn Darden on the set of
Indiangivers, Millbrook, New York, summer 1967.
Photo by Diane Dorr-Dorynek

"Angry Man of Jazz," c. 1974
Photo courtesy Atlantic Records

East 10th St, New York City, 1975. A
rooftop photo session with Sy Johnson.

Above: En route to the Newport Jazz Festival, July 4th weekend, 1971.
Photo courtesy CBS Records

Below: Miles Davis's observation: "Mingus is a man!"
Photo courtesy Atlantic Records

Mingus and a 6-piece band drove from Newport, R.I., to Lenox, Mass.,
July 4th weekend, 1971, to perform at the Music Inn.

Mingus and Susan Graham Ungaro on the road, 1973.
Photo courtesy Sue Mingus

Mingus in Japan, 1974. Photo by Sue Mingus

Mingus was at his peak recording *Changes One* and *Two* at Atlantic Studios, 19
Photo by Sy Johnson

Mingus at home, in an apartment on East 10th Street taken over from
Diane Arbus, 1975.
Photo by Sue Mingus

Mingus backstage, 1975. Photo by Sue Mingus

Mingus on tour, Kansas City, Spring 1977. Photo by Sue Mingus

Mingus and Susan Graham Ungaro Mingus,
Woodstock, N.Y., Spring 1978.
Photo courtesy Sue Mingus

Mingus during the recording of *Me, Myself an Eye*, New York City, 1978.
Photo courtesy Atlantic Records

MINGUS/MINGUS

Al Young

Part I

Precognition _____

It was 1960, the long summer I did a lot of hanging out around the West Village and the Showplace with Charles Mingus and the Jazz Workshop. Even now, thirty years later, I can remember with video clarity how much fun it was to go driving around with him in his brand new Detroit car, talking about anything we felt like. Of course, I was all ears and wide-eyed. To me, Mingus, then in his late thirties, was experience and brilliance personified. Oh, I knew all the stories about his temper, his anger, his volatility and violent streaks, and there were times when I knew better than to greet him even distantly. But Mingus mostly showed me his gentle, generous side. Usually he was like an uncle to me, but sometimes that avuncular side did a flip and he turned almost paternal.

So, perched here above this bar where the bass sometimes gets to be so loud I have to phone down and ask the bartender to lighten up, I might have to raise my voice at times in order to be heard while I tell about Mingus and the effect he and his music have had on my life. Somehow I sense, nah, *know* that Mingus himself will be overhearing all this; listening, the way he always listened to the world around and beyond him.

Just before we met, Mingus and drummer Max Roach, working with other outraged musicians, had staged their own mini jazz festival at Cliff Walk Manor, just blocks away from Newport, Rhode Island's Peabody Park, to protest the increasing banality of the Newport Jazz Festival. After scuffling for so long in relative obscurity, Mingus was also enjoying something of a hit record, a hit for jazz anyway.

"Better Git It in Your Soul" was a hot, gospel-flavored track, laid down in fervid, upbeat waltz time. It was from *Mingus Ah Um*, the same album enveloping "Goodbye Porkpie Hat," Mingus's tender tribute to Lester Young, which became a classic almost twenty years later, when Joni Mitchell set words to it. Even at that hour, in 1963, "Better Git It in Your Soul" was having more than a passing effect on the musical scene.

Aside from Fats Waller's wistful "Jitterbug Waltz," cut in the forties, I hadn't heard much jazz in waltz or 6/8 time. But suddenly Cannonball Adderley was recording Bobby Timmons' "Dis Here," Miles Davis was making his classic "All Blues" and Duke Ellington was writing the sound track for Otto Preminger's *Anatomy of a Murder*, which included another brisk 3/4 time pleaser called "I'm Gonna Go Fishin'." The waltzy, soulful, gospel jazz sound was hot.

Even I had put some homemade words to Ellington's "Fishin'" and worked the song into my coffee-house folksinger act. When I read the letter Mingus wrote to *down beat*, complaining about how he was being ripped off, I wondered about it for a long time. Not only did Mingus accuse Cannonball of plagiarism; he even went so far as to hit the popular saxophonist with the ultimate jazz put-down of that era: He accused Cannonball of playing rock and roll. All of this still tickles me.

But "Better Git It in Your Soul" (variants of which Mingus had also recorded under the titles "Wednesday Night Prayer Meeting," "Better Git Hit in Your Soul" and "Slop") was opening a lot of musical doors. Rumored sales figures of fifty thousand copies certainly seemed to qualify *Mingus Ah Um* as a bona fide jazz hit. I had thought the ahhh and ummm somewhat sensual—in a churchy kind of way (the celebratory, yea-saying Southern Baptist and African Methodist churches I'd been raised in)—until I learned that the LP's title had evolved from a Columbia Records executive's attempt to grammatically decline Mingus's name as if it were a Latin noun.

So I figured the royalties from *Mingus Ah Um* were helping pay for the sedan taking me home. The car radio was tuned to a station playing folk music.

"You play this stuff," Mingus turned and said.

"Yeah."

"So what do you think of this chick Odessa?"

"Odessa? Oh, you must mean Odetta."

"Whatever her name is. I went over to catch her the other night. She oughtta learn her instrument, man. I mean, I could put a clamp on my bass too, you know, and not have to learn to play in all twelve keys."

As always, Mingus was speaking in an urgent shorthand that sometimes took me moments to adjust to and translate. By the time I'd figured out he was telling me how little he thought of guitarists who use a capo to make it easy for them to play in keys they hadn't mastered, Mingus was staring at me as if to calculate how far I'd drifted from this earth.

"What do *you* think of her?" I asked.

"Oh, she isn't bad," he said. "She's good. I like her singing. You're good too, and I like your style. You're a poet."

How funny it felt to be riding around with him; it was strange and laughable, both. It felt good being back in New York, though. I was visiting that city every chance I got since I'd first hitched a ride there from Detroit when I was seventeen. The minute classes had let out in Ann Arbor, I had flown straight to New York. And I was strictly winging it, beatnik style.

That summer Janet Coleman and her friend Patty Sexton had rented a large apartment up on West Ninety-third Street, off Central Park West. That's where I was staying. Or, rather, that's where several of us were crashing. Us included Ron Rogers, an alto sax player, Bob Detwiler, who played tenor sax, the pianist Mike Lang, a bass player named Jim Wigle and guitarists Marc Silber and Perry Lederman. We had each either flown, driven or hitchhiked to New York from Ann Arbor.

Janet had handed me the keys and said: "Patty and I aren't ready to move in yet, so you guys can stay there for awhile—if you're cool."

Naturally, we all thought we were Coolness, Inc., even though no single one of us had been far enough around the teacup to know where the handle was.

As Mingus chauffeured me back up to West Ninety-third Street, I remembered the night when he'd mercilessly razzed my buddy Perry Lederman about playing the autoharp. An irrepressible young folk guitarist, just old enough at the time to legally get inside bars or clubs, Perry had gone with Mingus and me to the Five Spot one night to catch Ornette Coleman and Don Cherry, who were creating a sensation just then, making real big waves. I recall being impressed by the way Mingus had gone up to Ornette before we left the club to tell him how much he'd enjoyed what he'd heard, and to convey his good wishes to Ornette's band.

When we stepped outside the Five Spot, Perry—renowned lingerer, loiterer and a genuine character—whipped his autoharp out of its case and, right there on the street, launched into a chorus or two of "Make Me a Pallet on Your Floor," which he sang in nasal Brooklyn tones, halfway parodying himself.

Mingus listened patiently, then reached for Perry's autoharp.

"Let me see this thing," Mingus said.

Perry handed it over, looking as though he might be as proud as I was to simply be in Mingus's company.

"Hmm," said Mingus, inspecting the instrument. "So you push these buttons to get your chords, then all you have to do is strum?"

"Riiiight," said Perry, beaming.

Mingus shook his head and said, "Hmmph! Well, I knew it was a jive instrument."

"But, Mingus," said Perry, "it does take some skill to pick out a melody on it and keep the accompaniment going at the same time."

Mingus was not impressed, but Perry just happened to have a guitar on hand too. In a flash, he had the handsome Martin out of its case and was leaning against the building, guitar on his knee, studying Mingus's and my reactions while he finger-picked some shimmering, doleful blues licks, Lightnin' Hopkins style, in the key of D.

"Al," he said, "go ahead and sing a little."

Accustomed to singing at the drop of a hat, I cleared my throat and slid straight into song:

Uncle Sam ain't no woman
But he sure can take your man. . . .

"I like that," said Mingus, clearly more favorably biased toward me than he was Perry, which at first I didn't altogether understand. In fact, I remember thinking how Mingus's attitude toward Perry might've even been a little racist.

But Mingus elaborated: "Now, what Al's singing's got a little originality to it. And that's what you have to remember: Do your own stuff, and learn your instrument. Learn your instrument and do your own stuff."

I didn't have the heart to tell Mingus I'd lifted those lines off a Folkways record by New Orleans blues man, Blind Snooks Eaglin.

So, as far as Mingus was concerned, Odetta needed to woodshed some more; that is, practice that guitar of hers, even though she was a star.

"Yeah," he said, "I went over to catch her at this concert, and I couldn't believe the people packed in there. They love her!"

"She's something," I said. "When we got her out to Ann Arbor—"

"We?"

"The campus Folk Music Society. It was the first time Odetta'd ever played a college gig, and she was so nervous backstage, she was trembling. Still, she was a knockout."

"Well," said Mingus, "folk music is hot. Always has been. I listen to it. I listen to everything. You have to."

"That's what I love about your stuff," I said. "Listening to you is like listening to the inside of myself. You know, if the way I felt and thought could have music put to it, it would be your music. I can't wait to see the book you're writing."

"You'll see it," Mingus said.

Besides feeling funny, I felt clumsy. How do you tell someone who's been a hero for so long what you really feel about him? It was like being in the car with Mozart—and he was doing the driving!

The intellectual enthusiast in me wanted to say: You know, that's just what I like about your work. You do manage to squeeze in everything, and you reach out pretty far too, like a powerful radio. But whatever you do, it's always grounded. Grounded in tradition, in folk and blues and gospel and the sophisticated Mr. Ellington and in Bird and Diz.

Instead I said, "What's amazing is you're such a great composer, a leader and about the best bassist I've ever heard. And I know how hard that thing is to play."

"You play bass too?"

"No, but my father did."

"Oh, yeah?"

"Yeah, and I played it a little in junior high. I

mean, I was really the tuba player. But our bass player came down with the mumps or the chicken pox—I forget which—just when we had a concert coming up. So, since I was one of the few band members who knew how to read the bass clef, Mr. Krejci had me woodshed on bass for about a month, with a girl from orchestra giving me tips. Louis Hayes, the drummer, he was in that band. About all I managed to learn were the basic positions and where the notes I needed to play the music for the concert were."

"What were you playing?"

"We were doing Grieg's *Peer Gynt Suite*, and I even got to play a little bit of lead. You know, that part of 'In the Hall of the Mountain King' that opens up with the bass going: *boomp-boomp-boomp-boomp / boomp-boomp-boooooom / boomp-boomp boooooom / boomp-boomp-boooooom*—"

Mingus laughed and shook his head as if he might've been thinking about a similar experience from his own learning days. Back, say, when he was studying trombone, then cello; back when his sight-reading was suffering because his ear had been so astute.

The literary me wanted to say: What I'm trying to do is figure out a way to write like you play. Kerouac and those guys, they know that the secret to the American way of pouring your heart out is locked up and mixed in with this music. But there's all that intellectual literary tradition they have to

Al
Young

work through. I want to go straight for the soul and gut and night-and-dayness of being alive. That's what you do, Mingus; you absorb all the traditions but you don't let that keep you from telling your story.

But instead I said, "I knew we were gonna meet. Back when I heard those old Debut records of yours—'Precognition,' 'Extrasensory Perception,' 'Montage,' 'Paris in Blue'—I just knew it!"

Mingus said, "Is that what you want to do, play music? Or is it the writing?"

"It's really the writing."

"That's what I thought," he told me. "You've probably written the same way for a million years."

I've never forgotten the way Mingus said that; casually but with great solemnity. He even said something similar to Janet in a letter. His words are as unforgettable as our first meeting.

❖   ❖   ❖

EVEN THOUGH THE SOUND of Mingus seems to have always been there at the back of my head, buzzing along the arteries of my auditory nerves, there actually was an in-the-flesh first meeting.

It was that same summer, 1960, weeks before the night of his motoring me home. I'd been wandering around the West Village alone and on foot, looking for the Showplace, the club I'd heard about, run by a pair of brothers, devoted wholeheartedly to Mingus and his music.

By the time I found the Showplace, sweating and excited, it was mid-evening and Mingus was out there on the club steps in baggy pants and polo shirt, quietly grabbing a bit of what passed for fresh air in New York. Awed and skinny, I had trouble at first believing how portly he was. He sure hadn't looked that big in photographs I'd seen.

I somehow mustered the nerve to mount the steps and introduce myself, blurting out more than I needed to about how much I loved his music, racing all the way back to "Mingus Fingers," his featured arrangement and solo with the Lionel Hampton band on an old Decca record my father had. Then I blurted out the names of the Red Norvo Trio sides he had recorded on Discovery, singles he'd put out on Debut, the company he and drummer Max Roach founded. Then I talked about the *Pithecanthropus Erectus* album on Atlantic.

Mingus must've figured me for a simpleton—and perceptively—but he was kind and warm and led me up the steps into the Showplace to be his guest for the rest of that night.

And what a night it turned out to be! It was an elegant joint; what they used to call swank. Mingus seated me right down front, told the waitress to give me anything I wanted—and all I wanted in 1960 was beer, beer, gallons of the stuff.

Mingus introduced me to the Jazz Workshop, as

he called his band, and the current crop of work-shoppers. There was a piano on the stand, but nobody touched it, except Mingus when he wanted to demonstrate something to the rest of the players.

Between sets Mingus sat at my table and started telling me about a young woman, someone who had come in a couple of weeks ago to catch the band. To hear him tell it, one thing had led to another and, during a break, he had occasion to shake hands with this striking person.

"And, Al," said Mingus, "do you know what happened?"

"What happened?" I asked, still wrestling with whether to call him Charles or Charlie or Mingus or Mr. Mingus.

He grabbed my hand, placed it on the table, pulled his hand back, then slowly moved it close to mine.

"What happened," he said, "was sparks flew. That's right, sparks flew when I reached to take her hand. Man, that ain't happened to me since the fourth grade!"

Right about then, who should pop up to join us at table but vibraphonist Teddy Charles. Mingus introduced him to me as Teddy Cohen, saying, "He goes by the name of Charles but I call him by his real name, Teddy Cohen. Either way he's one of the best vibes players in the business. Excellent. Teddy's moving, though, moving on up."

And then Mingus told Teddy about the woman

who had stopped by and made sparks fly. That connection was still very much on his mind. As I recall, she was a Vassar student; rich and thin—Vassarlean, as he later expressed it in a song title. And because the *Ah Um* album had been doing so well, Mingus figured it would only be a matter of weeks before he might be able to support this sweet young thing in the manner to which she was accustomed.

Ah, males! Ah, chauvinism! Ah, jazz and oh, show biz! Ah, Mingus, Ah Um and ah, tensions and declensions; the Latinate beginnings and endings of ethnicized Western Civilization! The woman, whom Mingus and I speculated might be with the Scott Paper Towel dynasty, never showed up again. But when another beauty did, who reminded him of her, who had the same coloring and girlish appeal, Mingus put her through a blistering, bebop courtship and married her in a matter of days.

But this was yet to happen. For then, for that night, Mingus kept his eye on me and played his heart out with the amazing musicians whom I couldn't believe were right there on the stand, so close I could've reached out and touched them.

Tenor saxophonist Booker Ervin was sounding affectionately like Coltrane, and multi-reed player Eric Dolphy sounded to me like the way Schönberg or Stockhausen might had they come up black in the States, gigging in rhythm and blues and bebop bands.

Trumpeter Ted Curson was tooting through the

roof, as Ellington used to put it. And that drumming dandy Dannie Richmond—well, I later heard Mingus was the one who'd gotten him off tenor sax and bought him a drum set. There wasn't anyone like Dannie, who was always as immaculately attired as he was thin; practically ectomorphic, in fact.

When the band struck up "What Love," the jazz cutie in me automatically superimposed Tadd Dameron's "Hot House" over Cole Porter's "What Is This Thing Called Love" which was something of a bop flag-waver fanned by Charlie Parker and Dizzy Gillespie's sultry breezes. But I was wrong; Mingus's departures from Porter's scheme were so inventive as to make "What Love" totally original.

As for "All the Things You Could Be by Now If Sigmund Freud's Wife Was Your Mother," I knew Mingus was crazy enough about Jerome Kern's "All the Things You Are" to be capable of stretching that lovely song as far as it would go, chordally and rhythmically, and letting it snap back into place again, still spinning on its string in mid-performance like a Jacob's ladder yo-yo going, "Here we go loop-de-loop!"

"Mingusian" is the term I've concocted to describe not so much a thing or style or a sound as a way in which things happen, sonically or otherwise, when Charles Mingus is involved. It's all a sea the way his spirit washes and roars through me.

The night we met, for example, was purely Mingusian. For example, I still haven't digested what he meant that night at the Showplace when he leaned across the table and said, "I been working on a book, a long, long book about my life. And since you're better educated than I am, I betcha you could help me with it. You could help me write it right."

"When can I see some of it?"

"Any time, any time you got the time. How about tomorrow?"

"Tomorrow?"

"Sure, I'll give you my number and you ring me up and tell me when you wanna come over and we can get going."

"I'd be thrilled, Mr. Mingus, thrilled."

"Good. It's a big job, but I think I got something."

Tomorrow never came. It never happened; we never got to first base with this Me-Author-You-Editor idea of his. The following day and all the subsequent days and nights I tried to get to see that manuscript of his, Mingus—sometimes firmly, other times gracefully—blocked the way or froze on me.

I'd been thinking: Oh, boy, if I can have the honor and privilege of working on a manuscript by the great Charles Mingus, then surely I'll turn into some kind of writer at the James Joyce or maybe even the Jelly Roll Morton level. I had read Alan Lomax's book, *Mister Jelly Roll*, and taken it seriously. But Mingus just plain didn't want me to see his book. Not yet anyway. In fact, he later offered the same editing job to Janet Coleman, but he actually let her read the manuscript.

So, when Mingus dropped me off that night, and dawn was close to making its move on Gotham like some summery King Kong, I asked my hero once again, mainly for the hell of it: "So, should I call you tomorrow about dropping over to look at the manuscript? This would be a good time for me to read it. I really do have the time."

"OK," he said, "but call me at the loft first."

Spur of the Moment _____

Maybe nothing, except the spirit of what all the people were doing who'd gathered at Ann McIntosh's place that April night in 1970, was supposed to make sense. What we were trying to do was wish Mingus a happy birthday.

He arrived at Ann's house on West Nineteenth Street all by himself, reserved and intense. He was carrying an LP copy of the second volume of the 1964 *Town Hall Concert*, the benefit performance he'd given for the NAACP.

"Put this on," he told Ann, our host; a college friend and someone David Dozer once described as "a southern aristocrat bohemian from Maryland." But that had been David's tongue-in-cheek description of a devout cultural activist on New York's avant-garde music and theater scene. Ann had been working hard in that capacity since she'd settled in Manhattan after graduating from college at, yes, the University of Michigan, Ann Arbor.

Mingus pushed the album into Ann's hands. "It's not out yet, but they got a copy to me. Put it on. I can't wait to hear it!"

Though obviously tired, Mingus seemed as eager that night as any of his fans would've been to hear what he and his band had done eight years ago.

"So where's Sue?" Ann asked, referring to Susan Graham, the gifted editor and writer who had become Mingus's companion and manager by then.

Mingus made one of his actor faces and said, "I don't know where she is."

Ann said, "But you're supposed to be living together."

"We're still mad at one another," he explained. "Why don't you call her?"

There he was, on his forty-eighth birthday, April 22, 1970, hulking and looking so austere in his three-piece British banker's suit that Jim Forsht pulled me into a corner and said, "You know, if no one knew any better, they'd think the guy managed some jewelery store up in Harlem."

If there were any jewels glistening in Mingus's mind just then, they had to be either edible or drinkable. Or both. In fact, moments after he'd wolfed down fistfuls of hors d'oeuvres, communed deeply with the main courses, inhaled a salad, swigged two bottles of imported beer—one German, one

Dutch—and then, as if for reward, splash-poured himself a genial glass of Burgundy (or was it Zinfandel?), that serious look on Mingus's face disappeared.

Mingus might not like me talking about how he could eat, *greaze*, chow down, scarf. But what the hell! It's the jazzlike telling of this thing—and he knew this as well as I ever will—that thrills and swells.

The two or three times I'd ever seen Mingus thin, or straining to be—trying out thinness for good measure—he really would get evil. I suspect he had a hard time handling thinness. Was it because he couldn't stand how it brought out his movie star handsomeness? Maybe his shrink, Dr. Edmund Pollock, was the only one who knew for sure. "He is in great pain and anguish because he loves," Dr. Pollock once wrote of his patient in the liner notes to Mingus's 1963 album, *The Black Saint and the Sinner Lady.* "He cannot accept that he is alone, all by himself, he wants to love and be loved. His music is a call for acceptance, respect, love, understanding, fellowship, freedom—a plea to change the evil in man and to end hatred."

Whatever the reasons for his insatiable appetite for food, it was instructive to watch Mingus eat. For one thing, it made me wonder again about the bebop penchant for excess and substance abuse, for overindulgence; self-destructiveness, really. I loved this music so much, yet all my young life I'd been watching its originators and players die off prematurely. Long before his forty-eighth birthday, Mingus had begun to complain about the loneliness he felt now that most of his best friends—people like Bird, Fats Navarro, Bud Powell, Oscar Pettiford, Eric Dolphy and Booker Ervin—were gone.

Full at last, Mingus joined our informal story conference in the living room.

I said, "Since Ann's got all this new videotape equipment, why don't we do a show."

"That's an idea," said Ann herself.

"A terrific idea," said Janet.

"So what'll we do?" said Mingus.

"We can improvise a play, or something," I said.

Ann said, "Well, I'm not gonna be in it."

"Why not?" said Mingus.

"Because," Ann explained, "whenever I get in front of a camera, it's disastrous. I can direct. Or I can work camera. Hey, wait. Let's call Sue. Mingus, do you really mind if she comes over?"

Mingus looked away for an instant, then hunched his shoulders and said, "I don't care. Doesn't matter with me one way or the other. You wanna call her, go ahead."

While Ann was dialing, the rest of us went on talking about story possibilities. Janet, Jim Forsht, Ann and I knew each other from Ann Arbor; David had never been to Ann Arbor. But everybody in the room was into either language, the arts, the performing arts or all three. It was curious; something Janet and I would muse about decades later as we

wonderd why she and I had often been so defen-
sive, even apologetic at times, about the performing
arts background we shared.

All the same, creating a teleplay right there on the
spot was just the kind of thing she and David and I
could come in on early and stay late.

David said, "We ought to think about the show
we're going to do."

Janet agreed.

David and Janet were both professional, improvisational actors whose specialty was comedy. Their
experience with extemporized theater, with creating
scenes and whole plays from scratch, out of thin air,
often with invisible props, was extensive. It was easy
to understand why David, Janet and Mingus were so
crazy about one another's work; work that usually,
when it was done right, got transmuted into a kind of
play that depended on being in the moment.

On the sleeve of the *Mingus Ah Um* album, Mingus had written: "I 'write' compositions on mental
score paper. Then I lay out the composition part by
part to the musicians. I play them the 'framework'
on the piano so that they are all familiar with my
interpretation and feeling and with the scale and
chord progressions to be used. Each man's particular style is taken into consideration. They are given
different rows of notes to use against each chord
but they choose their own notes and play them in
their own style . . . except where a particular mood
is indicated."

"I've never met anybody more in the moment than Mingus," Janet insists to this day.

"When John Cassavetes was making *Shadows*," Mingus told us that night, "we didn't have a script. We worked it out one scene at a time, and that's how I wrote the music."

More Mingusiana, I thought, for his remark had been just the catalytic aside we must've needed to stir things up. It just so happened that David Dozer had lived in the very apartment where *Shadows* was shot, and out in California, where I'd emigrated by then, I had heard a little something about that film, considered to be very hip for the period.

Shadows was about a peas and carrots romance (interracial love; he's white and she's black), which Cassavetes had shot in 16 mm for well under fifty grand. When the movie had come to Berkeley's arty Cinema Guild and Studio Theaters on Telegraph Avenue—where Arl, my wife to be, worked taking tickets and researching movies for the husband and wife owners, Ed Landberg and Pauline Kael—I made a point of sitting through *Shadows* a couple of times, at least, to try and get a feel for the realness of what was supposed to be going on up there on the black and white screen in imaginary New York, when dreams were green.

"But I hear that script was only partly improvised," I said.

"Well," Mingus conceded, "John told us how the story was gonna go; the general, overall story line, but that was it. The actors didn't know what they were supposed to say from one scene to the next. We were all improvising; John too. But we weren't improvising off nothing. That's what made it exciting. We didn't know what we were in for, not completely."

Nor did we know what we were in for that night. But, I suspect, we knew we couldn't go too far astray, not with all those theater people on hand. Ann and Janet, along with their colleagues Lyn Austin and Ed White, had been soulfully holding together a lovechild of theirs called the Loft Theatre. The Loft is history now, but Saul Bellow's first play had been staged there, and novelist Norman Mailer had done his first improvisational acting, with enthusiastic encouragement from Ann and Janet, at the Loft Theatre.

Suddenly there we were about to improvise a little mini-drama right in front of Ann's new video toy.

I'd long known about Mingus's interest in acting. In a way, this interest in theater was evident in everything he did. The late multi-instrumentalist, Rahsaan Roland Kirk, a prominent member of the Jazz Workshop in the early sixties, used to say that Mingus taught him a lot about getting an audience's attention. And Kirk, who was about as eccentric and flamboyant a blind musician as ever there was, was telling us something!

A lot of Mingus the actor came out in "Passions of a Man," the strange spoken voice track at the end of the *Mingus Oh Yeah* album he put out in 1961. On it, Mingus overdubs voices and inflections on top of one another in his own made-up languages. You never really hear him say anything intelligible or in English, and yet all the moods and characterizations he has on his mind get powerfully and playfully conveyed.

Seated directly across from him, I could feel the quiet crackle emitted by his body as we talked over what this drama would be about.

When Susan Graham finally arrived, looking to me like a trench-coated, intellectual Simone de Beauvoir to Mingus's stodgy Jean-Paul Sartre, I watched how cool he tried to act toward her at first. It didn't last long. By the time Sue had taken off her coat and was sitting in cross-legged lotus position on the floor beside him, Mingus had loosened his tie and unbuttoned his vest.

"So does anybody have any ideas?" Ann asked.

"How about something in the suburbs?" Janet suggested, shining, excited, and as open to experiment as she'd been when we'd met in Ann Arbor almost fourteen years earlier; when she was sixteen and I was almost nineteen. "There's this triangle," she said, "two men and a woman, and—"

"No," said Mingus. "How come it's gotta be something about the suburbs and people sneaking around on one another? That's all we see on television day and night. Why can't it be about something different? Something more uplifting?"

Who was going to challenge that? Again, Mingus was casually influencing the direction of whatever was to come. There he sat, rejecting Janet's story idea before she'd even gotten it all the way out. And, to show how I felt about Janet, I automatically started feeling uncomfortable again about having sat on her first short story, "Chameleon," which she had shyly tendered to me when I was co-editing *Generation*, the campus literary journal.

"Chameleon" was about two high-school kids in Queens, a Jewish girl and a black guy who were dating. However, the girl had trouble accepting the guy, because he kept insisting he was more Jewish than she was. She wanted him to be accepting of his own ethnicity and culture. The story was serious, but it was also funny and crisp; a well-written piece of fiction, eventually published in *The Purple Cow*.

I'd sat on Janet's story because of general ideas I was developing at the time about civil rights and cultural ideology, but also because of specific ideas I'd had about how black people were supposed to be depicted in dramatic literature. Looking back, I can see how I was guilty of stereotyping myself and all other black people, the same way others still stereotype blacks, jazz, musicians, artists, the fifties, the sixties and imaginative styles of living. In other words, the black character in Janet's story had every right to be whatever the hell he needed to be.

But in 1958 I was so doctrinaire and theoretical that I'd messed up and missed the boat; missed the point of her story altogether. It's a wonder Janet even continued talking to me. I can now say that, even though I wasn't moving in orthodox circles, I still wanted to be politically correct and liked, so it isn't surprising that I ended up being a ham for love.

A lot of the ham canned up in Mingus came oozing out that theatrical night at Ann's. But it was his roommate Sue who finally got our impromptu teleplay off the ground.

"I've been reading this book by William Seabrook on witchcraft," she said. "And there's this chapter on Eskimo religion. Whenever the Eskimo want to seek out the spirit, they retire to certain caves and pray with one arm held up in the air—like this."

We watched while one of Sue's arms floated up above her head.

It got so quiet in the room that all we could hear was the sound of Mingus's *Town Hall Concert* playing in the background with great urgency on Ann's modest stereo.

"That's it!" said Janet. "We can do a sort of morality play, except it won't have to be so heavy."

Mingus smiled, and so did David. Ann seemed relieved, and I was pleased. Jim Forsht was off in the kitchen, pouring himself another glass of wine.

"Since you brought it up," Mingus told Sue, "you can be the Eskimo in the cave."

Sue, who was shy about our whole undertaking, said, "Oh, I don't know. All right, as long as I don't have to say much."

"We need a name for you," said Janet.

Sue thought for a moment. "All right," she said, "Chukfa. I'll be Chukfa, the Eskimo communing with Spirit."

"Hey, OK!" said David. "Let's just do it. If not, I can always do another episode of 'The Fat Chef.'"

At this, Mingus broke up because he loved David and Janet's comedy routines and already knew about "The Fat Chef." I didn't.

I was in town from California to give a reading at the Cooper Union, the Great Hall, where Abraham Lincoln once spoke. (Mingus, by the way, regretfully traces his ancestry back to Lincoln.) Because it had been scheduled during Passover, which also happens to fall at a time when most colleges close down for spring break, my audience had consisted largely of winos and other homeless types who'd come into the Great Hall to get out of the cold. What a gig! I still appreciate the instant compassion David and Janet expressed at that time for the predicament I was in. It seems they'd gone on FM station WBAI with a comedy act the night Martin Luther King, Jr., had been assassinated.

Anyway, the prospect of David doing another "Fat Chef" installment sent Mingus into belly-quaking spasms of laughter. For some reason, I wasn't connecting with the obvious affinity he would've had for the subject. After all, Janet wasn't the only one to rave about the toothsomeness of Mingus's fancy home cooking; his chicken and dumplings especially.

Granted, there was nothing fancy about our production, but it didn't take long for us to know we were cooking. When Sue as Chukfa struck that upheld arm posture, we knew from the charged silence she gave off that we were on to something.

So now it was time to go a few dramatic rounds with this thing right there on the spot. What it turned out to be was a little skit, painfully reflective of the times, about an Eskimo revolutionary trying to lift the people's consciousness and get them to overthrow their corrupt leadership.

I played the rabble-rouser, Janet a moderate who comes over to my side. Jim Forsht, who was working as an editor at *Senior Scholastic* magazine, played an incoherent, damn-near comatose victim of oppression who ended up lying on his back, muttering and moaning about how the powers-that-be had seduced and traduced him. Actually, Jim had sort of tailored the role to the fact that he was tipsy and very sleepy.

I was delighted that we were moving on this spontaneous invention at last. For years I'd acted in improvised radio dramas with friends on tape recorders. I loved it.

I think what might've made me glad to be in our little improvised drama that chilly night was the way Mingus flopped back on his cushion and watched Chukfa as if she might actually be the Eskimo Joan of Arc. Straight off the top, I can say that the way Ann was shooting Sue in moody Greenwich Village black and white was making me eager to want my extemporized lines to come out sounding believable. I wanted to be a good-guy revolutionary worthy of the disenchanted motorcycle outlaws Mingus and David were portraying.

Chukfa was the one, though. Maybe it was her high cheekbones or that flowing white blouse that helped Sue allow the role to play itself. She played Chukfa so luminously that to sit cross-legged, right after the take, and watch her die, stakeless and flameless, on the playback monitor, didn't seem to make much sense. But the way Sue persisted in holding that one arm in the air above her head, while she bowed her head and spoke, did make sense. Why? None of us had time to stop and figure it out. She was good, that's all. I could tell Mingus thought so too.

Once it became clear in the play that the Eskimo revolution wasn't going to happen, I'll never forget what Mingus said to David on camera: "Well, we might as well sit back, relax, have a drink, maybe shoot a little heroin and enjoy ourselves. There's no way we're ever gonna beat the bastards, is there?"

Years later I would wonder if, by that line, Mingus was expressing the essence of the bebop attitude, or simply ad-libbing what felt right for that moment. I've never forgotten the moment. Nor have I forgotten how wide Mingus's eyes grew, watching the playback on the monitor once we'd finished.

Watching Charles Mingus ad-lib his lines in front of the camera that night in 1970 made me remember how, in his Southern California youth, he had sometimes picked up pocket money as an extra in Hollywood movies. I couldn't help wondering what kind of part he might've played in the Bob Hope and Bing Crosby 1941 movie, *Road to Zanzibar*, which Mingus used to like to list among his official credits. I suspect he might've played a native. A lot of the black extras in those old Tarzan movies were jazz musicians. They called that kind of extracurricular work "sidelining."

When I asked Red Callender about it, the legendary bassist and tuba player and Mingus's old teacher and buddy said: "Sure, sure, all of us did a lot of sidelines. It's true, they wanted black people, and I having red hair, they always wanted to stick me in the back. And I discovered later that the Watusis were tall and had red hair. Those kinds of things still go on."

"But Mingus was so racially sensitive," I told Callender.

"Oh, yeah," he said, "but not back then. Sidelining paid good money."

That night at Ann's, Mingus said something else I'd heard him say again and again: "One thing they never taught us in school was how to talk. That's the one thing I regret."

"But, Charles," said Janet, "you and David were great."

"Yeah," said Mingus, "but I could've been better." Then he told me: "Man, you were good at that rabble-rousing. Reminded me of some of those street preachers and speakers I used to catch up in Harlem."

When Mingus had the time, he always complimented me—even on my singing. Whether he was doing it to be nice or not, I was never sure. Nevertheless, I welcomed his reassurances hungrily.

Whatever else I might've been up to in those days, I had reached the point as an entertainer where I'd have to either get serious and make a record, start getting myself managed professionally, or leave show biz altogether and settle down into writing, which had always been my not-so-secret love anyway.

All of us who'd helped create it would give anything now to have a copy of that tape. But because she later needed some blank tape in a pinch, Ann McIntosh recorded something else over "Chukfa," erasing it entirely.

And along with "Chukfa," Ann also erased the jumping, hand-held-camera footage David and I had shot to Mingus's records. For my part, I'd wanted to see what it felt like to try writing with light while riding his sound. What fun that was! David and I agree that it was something like doing a "video" before there was properly such a thing.

"In spite of all the shenanigans and fits and outbursts and rages," Janet says wistfully, "the guy was a lotta fun. Mingus was fun. Everybody forgets this."

Al
Young

Pithecanthropus Erectus _____

And now we come to that chorus in the jazz of all this where I get to blow a storytelling solo about some of the ways Mingus has always talked to me, both before and after he slipped out of his breathing cocoon of flesh and shed the pain that quickened his sad departure.

You can hear some of that pain and anger mixed in with joyful cries and yea-saying yelps and yesses and loving nostalgia seeping through the background and foreground of everything Mingus ever played or wrote. But it was the bittersweet joy that first pulled me into his world. Even in darkest adolescence, I was ready to jump for joy and jubilance any day.

Even though I know there's no way to truly end or begin any of this, I still have to play something about my own early inner life to give an idea of how Mingus's music couldn't help but affect me long before we'd met. Besides, when it comes to histories and biographies of black creativity, everyone's so used to hearing about rats and roaches and racists and fascists and crack and crack-ups and outrage and rage that the other side of the record never gets spun.

I was a skinny kid with a big head, big feet and great, sad-looking eyes that were actually overflowing with light and curiosity about everything under the sun. I was light on those feet too. The 220 and the 440 I could run in a flash, but the coach could never get me to sign up and practice and come to meets because I worked downtown after school at Sidney Hill Health Club, an exercise, massage and steam room gym for businessmen, mostly Jewish.

Al Wardlow and his brother Don and I were three of the five people who made up the crew there. Working under the watchful eye of a tall but paunchy Jimmy Rushing-looking guy named Gus, we shined shoes and kept the locker rooms, squash courts and steam rooms clean and picked up.

The fifth fellow was an older dude named Champ. Champ was nineteen, but he was already a Rosicrucian and lived with a woman almost twice his age. Champ was so hip, in fact, that I ended up naming one of the characters in my first novel, _____ 105

Snakes, after him. And, like me, Champ was too crazy about music, books, radio, ideas, languages and street life to become involved with sports.

As for friends, I was keeping company with people my own age who were already budding thugs, hustlers, junkies, cops, jailbirds, ministers, lawyers, politicians, athletes, gamblers, soldiers, scientists, intellectuals and show folks. I'm not saying a lot of my pals and buddies and close associates didn't go to work in the auto factories or in offices, or didn't teach school or become sociologists, dentists, lawyers or doctors. It's rather that far too many of them ended up either on the streets, behind bars, washed up before their time, or dead.

On the other hand, an equally surprising number of my schoolmates and neighbors went on to become celebrities and socially acceptable achievers in one field or another. Central High was like that when I was there in the early fifties.

Central was a totally atypical American high school, predominantly Jewish at just that moment, with a healthy and rising number of colored people—as we called ourselves then—and sizable sprinklings of other goyim. This included northern and southern whites, Italians, Czechs, Poles, Ukrainians, Armenians, Arabs, Syrians, Mexicans and a handful of Asians. The chemistry was sometimes overpowering. Anything could happen at any time—and usually did.

Saturdays—this was the eleventh grade—I

worked from morning to night at Sidney Hill with
the Wardlow brothers. Al played trombone in the
school band, Don trumpet, and I, like my dad,
played tuba and baritone horn. The happiest times
at the busy health club were when we'd be shining
shoes in a side room where Gus let us listen to the
radio, if we didn't play it too loud. The show we
were all crazy about was Dick MacDougall's "Jazz
Unlimited," which came all the way from Toronto
over the Canadian Broadcasting Corporation. We
picked it up over CBE Windsor, the CBC Ontario af-
filiate on their side of the Detroit River.

We always registered interesting reactions to the
records MacDougall would play, but it was Champ's
remarks that always drew my attention. I remember
listening with him to Monk's solo piano rendition of
"Just a Gigolo" while I was shining shoes for a
gentleman who always told me: "I expect a good
job from you, OK? Don't come giving me one of
those double-talking shines."

I almost doubled over with laughter while I
worked on those shoes. At the same time, I was
watching Champ concentrate on Monk's studied
version of Viennese composer Leonello Casucci's
old 1931 ballad.

Finally Champ said, "That's what I love about
Thelonious, man. Listen at that. Listen at how he
lays back and acts like he ain't sure which is the
right chord to play, so he hesitates on your ass
while you're waiting for him to strike the thing and

then—bam! Joker comes right down with one of those old homemade, far-out chords of his and it's right in tune and right on time. But in the meantime he's got us listening, don't he? Now, that's hip!"

That's the way I came up with jazz and through jazz and under the influence of jazz. Sure, it'd started with my father's playing and enthusiasm and that huge, rambling record recollection he'd carefully crated and brought up from Mississippi to Detroit, where he'd decided to settle after Navy duty in the Pacific. The music was always around; I could tune it out or tune it in, but it wasn't any big deal.

When *Pithecanthropus Erectus* came out, though, something happened to us there at Sidney Hill. We all had to look up from the shoes we were shining and take time out to do some serious talking about those shrieks and moans Mingus and his sidemen were hurtling at us along with all that new-sounding energy.

If I were a critic, I'd have to say it was Jackie McLean's sardonic, vibratoless ultra-bop cries and J.R. Montrose's festive, early Rollins-like taunts that put us away; that salted and peppered the musty, leathery, shoe-polish-smelling locker room air. But surely it was also the air itself; that is, breath leaking out of the mouthpiece and into the microphone and onto the records, and all that sappy, high-spirited, rhythmic, sexual crawling and strutting we heard—or were sure we'd heard.

At the time, Mingus said he was trying to capture musically how the first man must've felt who got up off of all fours and started to walk upright. Well, they don't call this link between man and ape *Pithecanthropus erectus* anymore; now it's known as Java man. But to a back room full of shoeshine boys in a Detroit health gym back in 1955, Mingus sounded as if he might've been sipping some strong coffee, indeed, to get all that down on a record.

This wasn't only head-turning music; it was dramatic, philosophical stuff Champ and I figured we only understood the half of.

"Damn!" said Don, "I can't even pronounce it, but they be *doing* that shit over there in New York, don't they? They just come right on out with it."

"At least Mingus does," I said.

"Sounds pretty prehistoric to me," said Champ. "That Charlie Mingus has got to be one crazy motherfucker. I'll have to go out and get that one."

"Shit, I'm going to New York," said Al Wardlow.

And, like the rest of us, Al did go to New York by and by. And he played his trombone with a lot of great musicians too; even did a long stretch in Sun Ra's Space Arkestra. He became a Muslim and changed his name to Al Hassan, but all of this had to wait while he put in his four-year hitch with the navy, which he joined right after we got out of Central High.

At Sidney Hill, Gus would get fed up sometimes and tell us: "Hey, I need some time off from that weird, crazy shit y'all be listening to. Get Bristo Bryant or 'Rockin' with Leroy' on that radio so we can hear us some Sonny Till and the Orioles."

Gus wasn't really all that nuts about rhythm and blues either, but it would do. His style was what we youngsters regarded then as hopelessly old-timey. Gus liked Savannah Churchill singing stuff like Buddy Johnson's "Since I Fell for You" and Bull Moose Jackson's "I Love You, Yes I Do." Or else he liked Nat Cole's "Nature Boy" or Saunders King's "Hambone." He liked anything by Dinah Washington or Lionel Hampton, but he got real nice whenever Ruth Brown's "Mama, He Treats Your Daughter Mean" came on the radio.

At the time, I hadn't known about the arrangements Mingus had done for Dinah Washington when he gigged with her back in 1945. I wasn't yet aware either that he'd played and recorded rhythm and blues as well, even though I did know about his recordings with Hamp.

"Mingus Fingers" had found its way into my father's sleeveless stacks of 78s. I was only eight when it came out, but later I tuned in to it and got to know it by heart. I understand Mingus had to get up off of a lot of rights to get that record out with Hamp. My mother knew Hamp and his wife Gladys. "Gladys used to drive the Cadillac," she told me, "and make Hamp ride in the bus with the band. And she used to drive a hard bargain too. Gladys was a businesswoman. I remember her from when I was friends with Joe Louis and Joe and Hamp would go out to play golf together."

Be all that as it may, Hampton does let Mingus take a long solo on "Mingus Fingers." And listening quietly, I can hear how even then, in 1947, Mingus had already developed his plucky, buoyant way of scoring for brass and reeds.

Up until Bird flew into his heart and nested there, Mingus's head had been turned by Duke Ellington and his fabled bassist Jimmy Blanton. He even took to calling himself Baron Mingus on some of those embryonic recordings he made in LA. And he was writing so much original music, much of which didn't get performed or recorded for decades.

For example, the very first music by Mingus I'd heard on record in the early fifties had been written while I was still crawling on all fours, or maybe just learning to walk.

Part II

Make Believe _____

One spring a thousand years ago in Detroit I walked into Mel's Record Shop on Twelfth Street and Angie, the blonde whose place it was, winked at her assistant, Willie Bolar (who would later join tennis player Althea Gibson's training crew), and said, "Al, I got in some new jams I'll bet anything you're gonna dig."

While I walked around, looking at the new releases whose covers graced Angie's wall display, Angie slipped the needle of her store phonograph into a 78 rpm recording of something called "Make Believe."

"Who's it by?" I asked.

"Charlie Mingus," said Angie.

In moments I was back at the counter, leaning across it, giving the music my uninterrupted attention. I could feel a bubble of adolescent happiness expanding inside me. Enthralled might sound corny, even phony, but that's what I was—enthralled. Thrilled, really. There's no other way to put it.

"You gonna play the other side?" I asked.

"There are six sides," said Angie, "and I've been playing them for days."

It was 1954 and Charles Mingus's "Make Believe," "Portrait," "Extrasensory Perception," "Precognition," "Montage" and "Paris in Blue"—all of them originals performed by him and by top-notch colleagues (with cellists and French horn players yet!)—were giving me the same feeling I still get whenever any kind of genuine joy goes percolating through my nervous system. This new music Angie was spinning and turning me on to—a little like bebop, a little like classical, a little like pop—was, all in all, like no music I had ever experienced before. It made me feel like living forever.

"Make Believe" was a Mingus ballad penned in the seedling forties and put out on his and Max Roach's Debut label in the harvest fifties, when I was a junior high school paperboy throwing the *Free Press* in Detroit's Northwest section, my lively, changing neighborhood. I was making so much money that I could mack real cool into Twelfth Street record shops like Mel's or Drew's, or the House of Music on Joy Road, or Grinnell's downtown and buy three or four ten-inch LPs or a Dagwood-sandwich stack of 45s or 78s, and feel no pain. Clerks like Angie (we all fantasized about Angie) would nudge one another and say, "Uh-uhh, here comes that boy that buys all them records!"

"Extrasensory Perception" and "Precognition" reminded me a little of the complicated Lennie Tristano records on Capitol I'd been studying: *Intuition* and *Crosscurrent*. But it was the plaintive, bluesy way Jackie Paris poured his Italian-American heart into "Make Believe" that had me grinning on porches for weeks thereafter, and dreaming through algebra, social studies and lazy, late afternoon lit classes, where we'd doze and mull and breeze and pore and snore over the classics. There I drifted, plugged into Mingus's world, dreaming about all the things I thought I was going to get done in this life, which, even then, was beginning to include writing a tribute such as this. To my ears the sound of Charles Mingus was like a voice uncoiling from within that filled me with a joyfulness directly connected to what Langston Hughes called "the Mystery."

It's impossible, of course, to pin down that sound in words. However, that sound did have a crazy tang to it. It was kind of like tasting some eccentric aunt or uncle's odd yet treasured barbecue sauce. Without that peculiar surprise ingredient he brought to it— let's call it that Ming quality of his; let's call it Ming— the music I was hearing Mingus perform could've been anybody's all-purpose, all-star, generic jazz.

But that little thing, that Ming made the difference. It could swing us, fling us, sting us or ding us, but mostly that bittersweet tinge with its unpredictable running-jumping-standing-stillness sound would somehow Ming us.

It was the lines Mingus had penned for Jackie Paris to sing on "Portrait" that warmed up something old and hidden in me:

> *The wind and the rain;*
> *The lull on the plain;*
> *O leaves on the ground,*
> *Mountain's gray brown, tipped*
> *With a dash of glowing white snow.*

And the lyric to "Make Believe," it's easy to see now, was ready-made for someone like myself—a late-blooming teenager, who read and read and probably thought too much:

> *People all say I'm dopey or they think I'm crazy*
> *And girls don't pull their hair out over me.*
> *But now that I've learned to make believe*
> *I'm as happy as a guy can be.*
> *You make believe with all the fine chicks*
> *And you're sure to get some crazy, way-out kicks. . . .*

If the words sound purple or simplistic, it helps to remember that Mingus was probably out to land himself a pop hit. After all, in the early 1950s records still weren't quite as tightly categorized as they would be in a few years.

For example, there was a disc jockey named Bob Murphy whom my buddy Leon Reynolds and I admired enormously. Murphy worked out of Detroit's WJBK and, because he was more than six and a half feet tall, he called himself "Tall Boy, Third Row." For his theme song, Murphy played a Boyd Raeburn number, an unusual choice in those days. Artistically, Raeburn was somewhat to the left of Stan Kenton, and anybody on the street, whether they listened to his band or not, would've told you Stan Kenton was too far out. But back then Murphy would think nothing of airing a Rosemary Clooney and a Sonny Rollins, or a Vic Damone and a Moondog and a Count Basie, or a Kay Starr and a Charlie Parker back to back. Delightfully eclectic, Murphy's taste was nonetheless impeccable.

I didn't categorize records, either, in those days. Like record shop dealers, my collector cronies were always sectioning their 78s, 45s and LPs into labeled bins—JAZZ, CLASSICAL, POP, R&B, FOLK, GOSPEL, FOREIGN, NOVELTY. I never went for that. To find whatever I needed, straight alphabetical filing by artist or title was good enough.

So, in addition to admiring Murphy and a host of other local deejays, Leon and I had our own shows too; plus our own radio stations, after a fashion. Leon's was WLMR, for his full name was Leon McKinley Reynolds. My station's call letters were _____ 119

WYSS, which stood for Young Sound Studios.

At the Hutchins Intermediate School print shop, Leon had printed us up business cards that advertised our respective side enterprises. For a modest fee, we'd come out to your home with our portable sound equipment units and play records for parties or other special occasions. I don't think either of us ever landed more than two or three gigs the whole time we were passing those cards out, but we were serious about it.

And we were serious about disc-jockeying too. I later went into radio for real and wound up for a spell on KJAZ, the San Francisco Bay Area's jazz station. But that's another chapter and verse; we're talking make-believe now.

There wasn't a day during this period when Leon and I didn't read to one another and compare the advertisements we'd written for restaurants, auto dealers, theaters and other businesses whose display ads we would study in the Yellow Pages of the telephone directory. Then, prepared with our records, ad copy, newspapers (for our news breaks), taped promos and announcements and, yes, our fervid imaginations, we'd sit in front of real microphones in our universe-rooms and conduct whole shows. We even each had a red light rigged up to the door and signs posted to warn unsuspecting household members and other uninformed visitors that they weren't to come barging in on us while we were on the air. Leon and I lived on the same street,

Edison, but he was four blocks east of me. We had no trouble keeping abreast of one another's styles and formats. There was always the telephone.

"Hello, this is WYSS," I'd announce once a record would be safely spinning and the mike clicked off. "And this is Al Young speaking."

"Hey, man," Leon would say, "You'll never guess what I just found out!"

"What?"

"You know that tune I use for my theme, Gene Krupa's 'Disc Jockey Stomp'?"

"Yeah, what about it?"

"Gerry Mulligan wrote that thing and did the arrangement for it when he was fifteen years old!"

"He did?"

"Yeah, while he was still here in Detroit, going to Catholic Central."

"How'd you find that out?"

"You know Miss Brownlee, our new English teacher? She told me. She went to school with Mulligan."

Miss Brownlee was the young beauty who used to drop by the back of the lit class while one student or another was up front giving an oral report. Sometimes she'd stay back there after classes ended and chat with me and Earl Williams, the drummer. Mostly we talked about music. She even knew about Mingus. Miss Brownlee wasn't much older than us, but she had a knowing, early-twenties take on life. She loved jazz, and yet she saw it as a problem.

"Hold on," I'd tell Leon. "I'm going on mike to introduce the next record. Be right back with you."

"All right," he said.

"That was the music of Yma Sumac," I'd say into my microphone, which was more than imaginary. "And now, plunging even further into the exotic, here's a brand new record by Charlie Mingus, one of the unacknowledged geniuses on today's jazz scene. We're going to hear a cut called 'Make Believe,' which will be followed up by 'Precognition.' If you've ever met someone or experienced something seemingly for the first time, yet you have this strange feeling that you've done this before or that you've always known this or that person— maybe from a dream or some other lifetime—then you know the meaning of precognition. But before we drift into the world of Charles Mingus, let's talk a little about Buddy's Bar-B-Q. I don't know about you, but I sure could go for an order of zesty, tangy ribs around now . . ."

And that was the way Leon and I carried on; that was one of the ways we played make-believe. Oh, we went on out with it!

After losing myself in those first Debut cuts, made in 1952 and 1953, I was a goner. Soon I'd be getting up for school an hour earlier than usual just to listen to "Reflections," the wistful, comforting ballad he recorded as a sideman with trombonists J.J. Johnson and Kai Winding in 1954. According to the album's liner notes, "Reflections" was from a ballet Mingus was writing then called *All About Love*. I still wonder if he ever finished it.

As a mystic, a Hindu, Mingus himself would've understood that none of this had up and happened out of the blue. Like a blithe and beautifying fungus, Mingus mushroomed inside me, killing off forever the notion that music or anything else had to go or be or stay a certain way. For years, I was going to be snickering to myself over this freeing realization.

It isn't easy describing or, more accurately, trying to recreate those early, sappy adolescent feelings of adventure, or that heroic sense of hurt that jazz in general and Mingus in particular brought out in me. As we mature, I suspect, we mostly forget what it's like to be new to the world. I agree with Kenneth Patchen in his *Journal of Albion Moonlight*, where he says that most people grow down, not up. That Patchen and Mingus, not to mention Langston Hughes and Mingus (all of whose work I discovered around the same time) should eventually team up at various times during the fifties to tour this country and Canada with their poetry and jazz acts also seems to have always been in the cards.

Kenneth Patchen was right, though. If we aren't mindful, we do grow down. Childhood and early youth get forgotten. We forget the kicks and rapture, those quick, fast-breaking and stretched-out thrills, the constant storming of heaven's gate, the continual awakenings, being in love all the time _____ 123 with someone or with something-or-other, the feverish pleasures of looking and listening, entrancement, voluptuous imaginings, breathlessness, and the all-protective notion that somehow you *are* going to live forever. And having so recently come into time by way of eternity, we know in those clumsy years more about forever than we do as we prepare to disappear back into that blissful native zone.

I want to sketch a pastel of what my inner life was like before Mingus. From what I've learned of Mingus's adolescence, he seems to have had similar growing experiences. And since the coming of age of America's black artists continues to be a subject that's rarely touched upon, I'll go another chorus or two to set the mood for what I myself was bringing to that moment when Mingus's path and mine finally crossed.

Mingus had been out of paradise longer than I had, yet the jolt I got when I first read the text he'd written for his early Debut extended-play 45s (with all of those numbers he'd composed in his teens: "Pink Topsy," "Miss Bliss," "Eclipse," "Blue Tide") had practically jangled with *déjà vu*. There Charles Mingus was, talking about "the many selves I have at my disposal" and God and things you simply didn't run across on the average LP liner sleeve. And it was saying something. Directly to me. It told me I was plugged into something so vast that—just like they sing about in the old Negro spiritual—you

couldn't get under it, you couldn't get over it and
you couldn't get around it. You just had to walk
through the door.

And this, the doors never stopped opening.

❖   ❖   ❖

MAKING FRIENDS WITH OLDER PEOPLE was nothing
new. Grown people, like the painter Harold Neal
and Jodi, his beautiful wife at that time, accepted
me readily while I was still in my mid-teens. Harold
worked as a lineman for Michigan Bell in Detroit,
but he and Jodi also edited the journal *Idioms*, published by the New Music Society, a rather valiant organization devoted, as we put it, to the propagation
of jazz and contemporary classical music through
live performances and recordings.

Every Sunday afternoon and Monday night, for
either fifty cents or a dollar, depending on whether
you were a member or nonmember of the New
Music Society, you could drop in to the World Stage
Theater in Highland Park and catch up to four hours
of music performed by top-flight touring musicians
and locals. But those "locals" included the likes of
Barry Harris, Charles McPherson, Lonnie Hillyer,
Kirk Lightsey, Roy Brooks, Louis Hayes, Donald
Byrd, Elvin Jones, Pepper Adams, Dorothy Ashby,
Alice McLeod (the future Alice Coltrane), Terry
Gibbs, Tommy Flanagan, Doug Watkins, Kenny _____ 125

Burrell, Curtis Fuller and Yusef Lateef. Drummer Louis Hayes, a bandmate of mine from junior high, used to say, "You come to Detroit, you had to know your instrument. If you didn't, you were gonna get cut. We even had a woman named Dorothy Ashby, who was one of the baddest harp players around, so you couldn't even get away on the harp!"

At the Neals' Atkinson Street home, I met so many legendary musicians it seems like a dream to recall the scene now. Yusef Lateef was one of them. It was a double treat to later hear Yusef Lateef on the Mingus LP *Pre-Bird*, breathing fire through his tenor, again lighting me up the way he always did when I'd catch him at the World Stage in Detroit back in high school. Yusef used to knock me out continually; not only when he played, but also when I'd stop by the Detroit Symphony Thursday nights on my little student discount ticket, which all the school band members could get. There'd be Yusef, stationed in the first balcony, in a dark blue suit, white shirt and tie, with a music score pad spread on his lap. He was getting his master of arts degree in music at Wayne State University and, as I gradually learned, was busy writing a symphony himself. It was because of Yusef that I took up the Qur'an, embraced Islam for about a year, became an Ahmediyyan Muslim, the sect he belonged to, and quietly went by the spiritual name of Ali Rahman.

Most important, Harold and Jodi and their friends—artists, intellectuals, scufflers, working people and lovers of music—accepted me for what I was.

"When I first met Al," the incurable bohemian Forrest Jones once said, "he was sixteen years old and talking so much shit, I had to stand back and take notes! I knew he was gonna do all right as a writer."

Ed Gunther was one of the *Idioms* staffers. He was also a chemist for the company that made Roman Cleanser, a popular brand of laundry bleach. And he had variously been a junkie and a bass player. He also knew how interested in writing I was.

"You oughtta seen that big blonde bass I used to have," Ed had told me often. "It was beautiful. I used to help the other cats lock Sonny Stitt up in the afternoon. We'd lock him up in his room and wouldn't let him out till night."

"How come you'd do that?" I asked the first time he'd told me the story.

"Aw," Ed told me, "you are sharp, but you're still awfully innocent. Hell, think about it. That was the only way for us to make sure the dude would be around for the gig that night! I mean, I loved Stitts, but the minute he would've busted outta that room in the afternoon, wasn't no telling when you'd ever see him again. Stitts would head straight for wherever the whiskey, the gin or the dope was. And then that was all she wrote! But, you see, I understood. I was doing speedballs myself, over there round the Bluebird. You know what a speedball is?" _____ 127

"Nope."

"That's where you mix heroin with a little cocaine and heat it up and, oooweee! Look out! That's what's called a split kick."

"Ed, why'd you quit?"

"Music or dope?"

"Well, both."

"I got off dope because it was fucking with the rest of my life. There I was at Wayne, getting my degree in chemistry, and using. And I was trying to do sports too, but every time I'd take a shower, I'd come down. Do you know how much it was costing me to be coming down all the time like that? Man, it was too expensive! Then, when I got married, my old lady said, 'Quit, or else!'

"It was Stitts, though, who speeded my retirement from the music scene. One night, right after a set, he told me I needed to learn to *play* that thing before I could go jumping up there on the stand with him. Al, the cat did me a favor. Sonny Stitt saved me a whole lotta embarrassment."

Ed Gunther had a big thick soup-strainer mustache and studied Schopenhauer and Kierkegaard and Hegel and Freud. After he'd read some poetry of mine and an essay I'd written about how jazz, like the poetry of Edgar Allan Poe, had gotten its first respectful recognition in Europe, from the French, Ed Gunther told me: "You'll become a good writer, possibly great. You know why? Because you're black and you've been hurt. That cry will always be in whatever you write. Listen to Duke, listen to Bird, listen to Miles, all the greats. That cry is always there in the background some place while they be telling their story. You know what that cry is? It's the human condition, that's what."

As lucky as I was to always have people encouraging me—from school teachers to the crowd of grown black bohemians who adopted me when I was a quietly troubled kid—I still cherish this unexpected remark of Ed Gunther's. That must've been what it was like for Mingus to have people like Red Callender, Lucky Thompson and the painter Farwell Taylor validate him.

When I listen to "The Chill of Death," written when Mingus was eighteen and going through all that yeasty ferment in Los Angeles, I'm convinced that what Red Callender tells me today about the open-mindedness of young musicians he knew during the thirties and forties is true.

"We never made much of categories," Callender said. "It was the writers who did all that."

Classical, jazz, pop—it was all the same; they listened to it all. And Mingus had obviously absorbed everything his Mill Valley painter mentor, Farwell Taylor, had opened him up to—meditation and karma yoga especially. I've never fogotten what Mingus told *down beat*'s Ira Gitler.

"'Writing came natural,' Mingus said. 'I heard things in my head—then I'd find it on the piano. Jazz to me was Duke and church but I thought all music was one . . . jazz, symphony. That's the bag I was working out of then . . . I learned through meditation the will to control and actually feel calmness. I found a thing that made me think I could die if I wanted to. And I used to work at it. Not death and destruction but just to will yourself to death . . . I got to such a point that it scared me and I decided I wasn't ready . . . And ever since, actually, I've been running because I saw something I didn't want to see. I felt I was too young to reach this point.'"

I knew this dramatic yogic experience of Mingus had taken place in 1939, the year I drifted back into the world. But it wasn't until I'd dipped into Robert Gordon's thoughtful book, *Jazz West Coast*, that I learned how Mingus had originally recorded "The Chill of Death" in 1947 for Columbia Records, who wouldn't release it. It was simply too weird and unmarketable, they thought. Influenced though he might've been by Debussy, Stravinsky, Richard Strauss, Arnold Schönberg and Boyd Raeburn and his true master, Duke Ellington, Mingus wasn't yet in a position to have much say in the matter. He certainly was not "the nigger Stan Kenton," as one of LeRoi Jones' characters refers to himself in *The System of Dante's Hell*, a novel.

And Bird himself, the all-night owl, the man Mingus alludes to as "King Spook" in *Beneath the Underdog*, had been right there in the studio, telling Mingus how good it was; the sleepless Charlie Parker who used to call Mingus up sometimes and,

over the telephone, blow his alto saxophone to
Stravinsky or to Bartok records whirling in the background. Over the telephone! Was that where Mingus picked up his habit of calling people like Nat
Hentoff in the middle of the night and playing new
compositions on piano? Over the phone!

Oh, Lord, Don't Let Them Drop That Atomic Bomb on Me_____

To take things even further in the mystical direction, I was also one of those kids who stayed up late at night, beyond bedtime; an undercover listener to my compact Arvin radio, the metal model. One of the people who would turn up regularly on that hot little instrument, habitually after 11:00 P.M.—first from Cincinnati, then I started getting him out of Chicago and finally out of WOR, New York—was Jean Shepherd. Aside from my Uncle Billy down in Jackson, Mississippi, I thought Shepherd was one of the most wonderful talkers and story-tellers I'd ever heard. This was long before people started calling him a "radio bard" or a "hip raconteur."

By the time Mingus and Shepherd got together in 1957 and put out a narrative-and-jazz album called *The Clown* for Atlantic (on which Shep improvises on a story line Mingus had provided), I had escaped into college. It was there at the University of Michigan that I met David Newman. David edited *Generation* after Marge Piercy and before Ann Doniger and I took over. After that, he went on to edit *Gargoyle*, the campus humor magazine. When David left Ann Arbor, it was to work at *Esquire*. He also wrote a column called "Man Talk" for *Mademoiselle* for awhile before settling down to write a little picture called *Bonnie and Clyde*. That was before he'd gotten around to making his old undergraduate dream come true by writing all those smashing *Superman* movies in the seventies and eighties.

If I'm not mistaken, David Newman was the first person I'd met at Michigan who knew much of anything about either Mingus or Jean Shepherd. Like me, he loved them both. The difference, however, was that David had long been catching Mingus in person at such New York places as the Cafe Bohemia and Birdland. Moreover, David's brother was a professional actor who'd been in movies, TV and radio. I was impressed. David and I used to sit up nights at the Student Publications Building on Maynard Street, where our textbooks and notebooks lived in desk drawers. We often talked about bebop _____ 133 while we imbibed hot, machine-dispensed bouillon (which David called "chicken drinks") and whistled duets on the standards and jazz numbers like "Bernie's Tune" and all the learnable Monk and Bird tunes.

The United States was in the middle of the so-called cold war. My telephone was being tapped. I mean, my roommate Bill McAdoo, an up-and-at-'em radical, and I sometimes wouldn't pay our phone bill for months, but service never got cut off. The psych department—or so we'd been told by a campus editor, himself an informant—had a contract or an agreement of some kind with the FBI to get graduate students to spy on "deviates" like us.

Like any good deviate, I was circulating petitions for a sane nuclear policy, boycotting Woolworth's, marching on Washington, serving on committees, singing at rallies, where FBI agents would be waiting far out front with their long-nosed zoom-lensed cameras to snap pictures of the participants.

I was listening to Mingus, to Basie, to Duke by the ton (my folks and all the oldsters had plenty of Ellington on their record shelves), to West Coast jazz, to Stan Getz and Bob Brookmeyer, Woody Herman, Paul Desmond and Dave Brubeck, Gerry Mulligan and Chet Baker. And I was listening to hard bop, to Jackie McLean, Gigi Gryce, Sonny Rollins, Thelonious Monk, the stuff Miles was doing with Coltrane, Cannonball Adderley, pianist Bill

Evans and arranger Gil Evans (my ears told me that

Gil Evans, Monk and Mingus had all graduated with honors from Ellington University), to Clifford Brown and Max Roach, Art Blakey and the Jazz Messengers, Horace Silver and Ray Charles, Muddy Waters, Little Walter, Howlin' Wolf, Big Mama Thornton, Billy Ward and the Dominoes and other dangerous music. In general, you might say, I had either a hand or a foot or a finger or toe in the door of everything that showed the McCarthyites, the Dixiecrats and all the other neo-fascist racists and rascals where they could go. And also what they could do with their Brave New World and their Animal Farm all rolled up in one; their neo-plantations of the mind.

When I first saw the title "Fables of Faubus" on Mingus's *Ah Um* album, then listened to it, I had the eeriest feeling that there was more to this piece of music than met the ear. The melody had such an aggressive thrust to it, and the bridge, with Jimmy Knepper's smearing, jeering trombone, was so intriguing that I thought there just had to be words to this thing. "Fables of Faubus," what did that mean?

It was Jim Forsht, a Korean War vet from Pennsylvania, a writer also, who told me that there were words to this Faubus thing. Forsht lived next to me in a bay-windowed house on East William Street. He loved Fitzgerald, Hemingway, Robert Benchley, Bruckner, Shostakovich, Bartok, the French horn playing of Dennis Brain, Lerner and Loew's *My Fair Lady*, Leonard Bernstein's *West Side Story*, hot pizza _____ 135 and jazz (pretty much in that order). He'd heard the Mingus Jazz Workshoppers sing "Fables of Faubus" during a Christmas trip to New York.

"I couldn't really understand them all that well at the club," he explained. "But I could tell they were political. You'd really like them."

What interested me about Governor Orval Faubus wasn't his calling out the Arkansas National Guard to keep the black kids out of Little Rock's Central High School. Pro–Jim Crow politicians in the South were fully expected to defy the 1954 Supreme Court decision.

Here's what I found curious about Faubus. Word had somehow trickled down to me that the infamous governor had attended the Highlander Folk School in Arkansas, the same blacklisted institution that, according to its right-wing opponents, had given us such despicable conspirators as Pete Seeger, whom we college kids adored for his crusty idealism and defiance of the House Un-American Activities Committee; Guy Carawan, who wrote "We Shall Overcome," the theme song for the Civil Rights Movement; Dr. Martin Luther King, Jr., and more communists than you could fit on the dome of the Kremlin.

Just as Mingus had told me in the early seventies that at least one of the Black Power Movement's higher-ups was drawing checks from a Swiss bank account set up by the CIA, so I'd heard way back in the late fifties that Orval Faubus had originally been, shall we say, more left-handed than he was right-handed where the give-and-take of social awareness was concerned. On such hearsay, provable or not, I concluded that one of his hands must've known what the other was doing.

Columbia Records wouldn't let Mingus perform the lyrics to "Fables of Faubus," so he got the worded version out on a smaller label, on Candid. Of all people, Mingus certainly must've already known that Billie Holiday, in the 1940s, had to go to Milt Gabler's storefront Commodore label to record the poignant "Strange Fruit." Columbia didn't want to have anything to do with such a troubling, anti-lynching song.

Pundits may be arguing about Mingus's politics for centuries, and the titles he gave his compositions should be enough to keep their fires fueled. Besides "Fables of Faubus," there is "Prayer for Passive Resistance," "Cry for Freedom," "Meditations for Integration," "Meditation on a Pair of Wire Cutters," "Charlemagne," "Once Upon a Time There Was a Holding Corporation Called America," "Remember Rockefeller at Attica," "Free Cell Block F, 'Tis Nazi USA," "Smog LA," "Freedom," "Please Don't Come Back from the Moon," and one of my favorites: "Oh, Lord, Don't Let Them Drop That Atomic Bomb on Me."

In Europe, Asia and other parts of the world, people seem to be more sensitive about nuclear warfare than we are in North America. Since the

1950s, when we lived with the idea that it could blow up at any moment, I've deeply wondered about our indifference. With all of those strategically placed Russian and American missiles waiting to be activated all over the globe, how is it possible, I've wondered, to keep ignoring the fact that we truly are all members of one another?

When Yuri Andropov replaced Leonid Brezhnev as Soviet leader in 1982, word spread quickly that Andropov was a Miles Davis and Dizzy Gillespie nut. Right away I began to conjure up images of Andropov kicked back nights with a chilled liter of vodka, munching on a boiled potato, blasted out of his mind as he took yet another bracing seaside stroll along Miles' "Green Dolphin Street," or parachuted once again down into Gillespiana Land to spend "A Night in Tunisia." And I kept thinking: How can you harm a people whose culture produced the music you love?

I can't listen to "Fables of Faubus" without doubling back in memory to Woolworth's and the picket lines we walked in the late fifties. That vaudeville-sounding Mingus tune carries me back to all the fear that hung in the air of everyday college-level discussion during the McCarthy era, when professors and students feared the presence of FBI agents in the classroom. "Fables of Faubus" takes me back to the 1959 March on Washington and the carload of us who drove there from Ann Arbor and, while waiting to hear Harry Belafonte sing, almost got ourselves stomped to death by uncool mounted policeman right there on the Washington Monument mall.

"Oh, Lord," Mingus sang, *"don't let 'em shoot us! / Oh, Lord, don't let 'em stab us! / Oh, Lord, no more swastikas! / Oh, Lord, no more Ku Klux Klan!"*

We didn't know then that the FBI was trailing Louis Armstrong because of a letter he'd written to President Eisenhower suggesting that marijuana be legalized. But I can tell the world that it was comforting to be jazz-crazy at that warped bend in time and to hear some of what was going on socially and politically getting expressed in the music.

I can also attest that the Jazz Nazis, those invincible legions of unreconstructed jazz purists— whose number boasts more bureaucratic archivists than open-eared lovers of music—couldn't stand Mingus.

"When I go to listen to some jazz," one professorial old-timer told me around 1960, "I don't want to hear all that Greenwich Village, left-liberal, protest shit! I'm shelling out to hear some sounds, man! Don't care what you say, they couldn't be talking that stuff in Russia. You know why? 'Cause Stalin told 'em back in the thirties that jazz was a decadent, bourgeois, capitalistic music. And, dammit, that's the way I want it to stay!"

"Well," I told this loudmouth, whom I knew to be a Catholic, "the Vatican hasn't exactly taken a favorable position on jazz, either."

"Yeah," he said, "and I like that too. That's exactly why I love it—it ain't respectable. Hitler didn't dig it, said it was nigger and kike music. The Central Committee and the Reds can't dig it, and now the Pope don't dig it. But you and me, hey, we can dig it."

That's the way it was in those days, when there wasn't any Black Studies. As a grade-school kid downsouth, I had learned more about the richness of black achievement than we were ever taught upnorth. And yet, all over the country, people who cared about music, reading, writing, painting, sculpting, dancing, acting and ideas, they got into all of those arcane areas: how the National Socialists and the Marxists and the Church of Rome felt about jazz.

Sure, I studied, steadily, and made the most of any information I found sitting around, whether on my own or in a formal classroom. But most of the black thinkers I knew simply put things together as they went along. That's what I loved about the creative spirit of jazz, which borrowed from every other living musical idiom and scource, and Mingus, whose zest for life itself was as strong as his insistence upon the right to free speech.

"We didn't work this music out in smoky clubs and bars," Mingus told poet Kenneth Rexroth. "We worked it out in people's homes—and we didn't call them pads, either."

And of Bay Area jazz columnist and broadcaster Phil Elwood, Mingus asked: "Why did Fats Waller's son kill himself? He was a good tenor player too.

Sounded something like Sonny Rollins. I saw the house out there on Long Island. Why did one of America's greatest songwriters die in such poverty?"

In 1963 I got hold of solo piano album, *Mingus Plays Piano: Spontaneous Compositions and Improvisations.* You could've heard me chortling and chuckling for blocks when I listened to his "Compositional Theme Story: Medleys, Anthems and Folklore." That is where Mingus, by then deep into his homburg-sporting, British banker period, interpolates—toyingly at first, then joyfully—"My Country 'Tis of Thee" into James Weldon Johnson's "Lift Every Voice and Sing." Back in my Mississippi days, when we sang it every day at our all-black school, we called Johnson's piece "The Negro National Anthem." By and large, it wasn't until Black Power came into style that northern-reared black people knew anything about "Lift Every Voice and Sing." But it soon got to where you couldn't go to a party or a benefit of any kind without hearing Nina Simone's or Ray Charles' recorded versions of it.

Again, there was Mingus, back there in the 1950s of blacklists, beatniks and bomb shelters, singing: *"They brainwash, teach you hate / And send you out to segregate."* And doing it to a melody and rhythm so captivating that the music and words still sound as fresh and as meaningful at the gateway to the twenty-first century as they did during the Eisenhower era.

Myself When I Am Real __

I didn't get into yoga until the early sixties, but so much of my experience up until then had been pointing in that direction. Islam, my fascination with Eastern thought and philosophy, with poets like Li Po, Omar Khayyam and Rumi, Jean Toomer, James A. Emanuel, the Zen craze of my college days—it all started coming together. I would even include in that list the cautious trying out of lysergic acid (the real thing, straight from Sandoz Laboratories in Switzerland) back when I was a lab aide in Richmond, California. A year later, full of peyote cactus, I spent a century-sized morning listening to Thelonious Monk play "Brilliant Corners" and "Don't Blame Me." I heard it in what Keats called "silence and slow time." It was then that I seem to have grasped why Marxist music critic Sidney

Finkelstein had given one of his books the title, *How Music Expresses Ideas.* All of this helped me understand that I was basically a happy, truth-starved person, and fundamentally pretty straight. I also learned that sound, especially in the form of music, played a shining role in my spiritual development.

In 1967 I sat down and wrote a poem, which I named after one of Charles Mingus's spontaneous piano solos. Naturally, I dedicated it to him.

MYSELF WHEN I AM REAL
for Charles Mingus

The sun is shining in my backdoor
right now.
            I picture myself thru jewels
the outer brittleness gone as I
fold within always. Melting.

Love of life is love of God
sustaining all life,
                    sustaining me
when wrong or un-self-righteous
in drunkenness & in peace.

                    He who loves me
is me. I shall return to Him always,
my heart is rain, my brain earth,
but there is only one sun & forever
it shines forth one endless poem

*of which my ranting, my whole life
          is but breath.*

                  *I long to fade back
          into this door of sun forever*

I even had the nerve to send a copy of the poem
to Mingus in New York, figuring, well, here goes
nothing. And for a long time, I heard nothing back.
Then, one October morning I got a postcard from
Mingus. It confused me at first because it was
signed Charles Mingus, Jr. But what it said was:
"Dear Al: I remember a beautiful young man who
wrote stories and poetry and who was in love with
life; he even played a little music himself. Take care,
Charles." The card had been postmarked in Berkeley, which confused me until I remembered that
Mingus always stayed with a certain family there,
people he had known from early youth. Asking
around, I found out that he had slipped into the Bay
Area to catch his breath and to look in on his old
friend and mentor Farwell Taylor. I was touched
that Mingus had taken the time to say hello. And,
when I saw him perform several months later at San
Francisco's Both/And Club on Divisadero, I told
him so.

    "What're you doing these days?" he asked.
    "I'm on a fellowship at Stanford."
    "Oh, yeah?"
"Yeah, it's giving me time to work on a novel."

"What you gonna call it?"

"Snakes."

"Hmm," he said, lapsing into the contemplative mode and shaking his head. "Good title. You already got me wanting to see what it's about."

"What's happening with *Beneath the Underdog?*" I asked.

"Oh," he said, "I finished it. Now I'm fooling around with these jive publishers."

It wasn't long after this that I saw the movie, *Mingus*, made by filmmaker Tom Reichman as his graduate thesis at New York University. I didn't feel comfortable sitting in the San Francisco audience, watching my artist friend Mingus get evicted from his Bowery loft. I dug Mingus's digs, although I never got to see the Bowery loft except in Reichman's film.

Still, it was fun to go back pictorially over the times I'd visited Mingus on Third Avenue and West Twenty-seventh Street. There hadn't been that many visits—maybe three or four. Still, in each visit something dramatic had transpired. Had those little dramas taken place exclusively inside my head? Perhaps. I was easily impressed. It was a treat just falling up there, as we would've said in those days, and catching an hour of trumpeter Hobart Dodson, working out some tricky ballad with Mingus at piano. Walking around and looking at all of Mingus's books, LPs, tapes, posters, scribbled notes, score paper scrawls, photos, pinups, bebop knickknacks and memorabilia put some kind of charge on me that crackled, I like to think, beyond the fatuous constraints of fandom.

For example, the pay telephone installed in one corner of his loft told me a lot about Mingus's feeling toward musicans and other visitors who came up there and needed to make a phone call. There was the fancy chess set, the typewriter, his collection of smoking pipes, his basses and, of course, the piano. I got the impression that there were periods when Mingus lived at that piano the way Thelonious Monk is said to have glued himself for days and nights on end to the upright piano he and his wife Nellie kept in their kitchen.

Mingus's Third Avenue loft was a world; a little city in itself. I remember running into Freddie Hubbard up there, and my old drummer friend from Ann Arbor days, Omar Clay. Mostly I remember presences and absences; the spirit of the place. Perhaps because it had originally been set up as a health gym—complete with slant boards, exercise equipment, juice extractor and a dance and workout floor—the space had something about it that was soulfully athletic yet, at the same time, meditative. It could just as easily have been a karate parlor or an indoor archery range.

Straight out of Eugene Herrigel's *Zen in the Art of Archery* is where Mingus and so many grand improvising performing artists of his caliber could've come from. I wonder if he'd ever read that book.

Knowing Mingus, he probably had. A lot of Charlie Parker's exponents were unpredictable readers. Max Roach once told me about how Bird would get himself a stack of paperback books, find some place to nod off after he'd finished a gig and gotten high, then sit up all night, reading and dozing.

"Bird knew everything," Art Blakey, for whom jazz is religion, still insists. "He could tell you about world affairs, politics, history, art, religion—everything."

I know the teenage Mingus made his way through Freud's *Introduction to Psychoanalysis*, and one of his endearing extramusical aspects was that he seemed to be an avid reader and writer. But it's only a hunch I have that tells me he at least flipped through *Zen in the Art of Archery*. Once Herrigel's Japanese archery master, who was also a swordsman and Zen Buddhist, had brought his baffled student to the point where he could begin to get himself out of the way and allow that elusive presence known as "It" to do the shooting, Herrigel discovered for himself how "bow, arrow, goal and ego all melt into one another, so that I can no longer separate them. Even the need to separate them is gone."

I thought I'd absorbed what this classic little text had to say back in the fifties; back there when *Evergreen Review*, D.T. Suzuki, Zen Buddhism, Alan Watts and Eastern wisdom—as distinct from Western knowledge—started seeping, then spreading across the land through what are now respectable, collectible beatnik channels. Recently, however, _____ 147 when I went back through Herrigel's narrative again, I couldn't help thinking of Mingus and his personal fling with archery.

In fact, after absorbing Herrigel's book in the full bloom of middle age, I couldn't help ringing Janet up in New York and telling her how I was willing to bet that the idea of being skillful with a bow and arrow appealed to Mingus because of his lifelong devotion to the double bass.

"Hey," she laughed, "I bet you're on to something."

"Think about it," I said. "Imagine what Herrigel, an uptight, left-brained Westerner was up against when he turned up in Japan to study archery under a Zen master. Think what he had to overcome; all that intellect he was so proud of. He had to learn to let go. Letting go of the chattering, so-called rational mind so the higher self can get through—that's gotta be one of the hardest things for a traditional Western person to do, don't you think?"

"I know I'm still having trouble with it," Janet said. "Like, right now, I'm struggling to finish this book on the Compass and improvised comedy. It's driving me nuts. And I've got all these resources—acupuncture, an herbalist, Al-Anon, my screaming class."

"Screaming class?"

"It's really called Bioenergetic Movement, but we learn to scream in there too. I need everything I can get."

"Why don't you invoke Mingus to help you. You *know* he's around."

Janet paused and said, "That's a terrific idea."

"Seriously," I said, "I got off the plane last night from New York, got in the car to drive home, snapped on the radio and there was Mingus. The guy was saying, 'For the past hour we've been listening to music by Charles Mingus.' Then after I'd barely gotten enough sleep to drive down to Santa Cruz to teach my screenwriting workshop, I snapped on the radio again and they were playing 'Better Git It in Your Soul' and 'Fables of Faubus.' I couldn't believe it. Well, actually, I *could* believe it. It all started happening right after he died. Janet, can you remember what you told me when he died?"

"No, what?"

"You were crying and you said, 'There goes our youth.'"

"I said that?"

"Yeah."

"Well, sooner or later we had to let it go. Letting go is still hard for me, though. The only time I seem to be able to do it is when David and I are doing comedy."

"Well," I said, "you know what it's like for an improvising performer to have to come up with stuff night after night after night."

Janet's voice started quavering again. "Mingus, he was something, wasn't he? We were so lucky to even be in his presence the way we were."

"You might want to check out Herrigel's book. In there, even after he learns to release the arrow and _____ 149 let it guide itself to the target, he can't help feeling proud."

"So what happens?"

"So his master chides him about the dangers of taking credit for something that he hasn't done; something that's been pulled off by a higher power."

Janet laughed again. "The guy was magic, wasn't he? I always half suspected he knew we were gonna grow up and write about him."

"Really?"

"Yeah."

"Well," I told Janet, "I kinda thought so too. I loved the guy."

"I loved him too," she said, barely able to steady her voice.

What Love _____

"What Love" might just turn out to be my favorite Mingus ballad. It's the faintly complex yet amazingly tender piece the Jazz Workshop was mastering and exploring that season when I first walked through the door. Back when, night after night, I'd watch a lovely portion of jazz history being made.

There was the night Candy Finch, a Detroit player, came in, just a few hours ahead of my Ann Arbor pal Omar Clay, to audition for a drum position rumored to be opening up. Mingus had put out the rumor. But Dannie Richmond, as it turns out, wasn't ready to split yet. Finch, who evidently had listened carefully to Mingus's old fifties version of "A Foggy Day," came to the Showplace with a batch of whistles, the kind Brazilian musicians use for rhythm, as well as a selection of penny whistles and old-fashioned slide whistles. When Candy Finch whipped out one of his whistles, thinking himself to be the thorough Mingusian, Mingus stopped playing bass just long enough to reach over and snatch it from him.

I was also there the night Mingus was auditioning bass players. Who should turn up but Ron Carter one night and Doug Watkins the next. Mingus, who was deep into piano-playing at the time, picked Doug Watkins. He even seemed to take some manner of perverse pride in telling people, "Yeah, I even got Doug Watkins on bass." He brought Doug out to the West Coast.

I like to think of "What Love" as Eric Dolphy's answered prayer for a vehicle that would allow him to run rife with his daring approach to improvisation.

Eric played so hard and with so much passion and tension, it was always a relief to watch him step back and rest after he'd gotten through the labyrinthine chordal structure, beautifying it *en route*. Nights at the Showplace, in the West Village, I used to get a kick out of watching him flirt with Tanya, Ann McIntosh's dark-haired, dark-eyed, dark-stockinged cohort from Baltimore.

I also remember Eric as someone who practiced all the time and, when he wasn't practicing or on the gig, he played the horses. Sometimes I'd stop by the Five Spot in the late afternoon, on my way, say, to McSorley's Saloon for cheese, crackers, onions

and my beloved ale, or maybe while I was just
making the rounds. That's where Ira Jackson, an
alto sax player from Detroit, who used to stay at the
Sloane House Y in Manhattan as I did, introduced
me to Eric and to pianist Barry Harris.

Barry I already knew from the Detroit scene, and
Eric, of course, I'd sort of gotten to know from
hanging out with Mingus. As the two of them stood
before me, courteous, friendly, fondling their copies of the *Racing Form*, in the somber light of the
moving moment—this would've been the happy-
go-lucky summer of 1960—I thought about Mingus
and all the musicians and painters and poets and
artists of all kinds I loved and had been learning
from since childhood, going all the way back to
Mississippi, my father and all the fathers I thought
I'd never had.

Also, it's always funny when you know someone by the way they chord a piano or fill a canvas
or turn a phrase on paper, then you find out they
do things like play the horses or chase women or
slip down to the Ho-Ho Dinette on Mott Street in
New York's Chinatown for *shaishu bau*, pork bun.
Or they're into wanting everybody to think that if
they weren't a gifted musician, turning the world
inside out and all around with sound, they'd be
turning out women, artfully pimping or trying to be
the number one pool shark on earth. That was Jelly
Roll Morton's specialty, so they say. And Coleman
Hawkins' name crops up too sometimes. What

would you call it? The artist as elegant lumpen proletariat?

It was a curious pose for Mingus to adopt. He wrote about it winningly in *Beneath the Underdog,* especially when he spoke about Billy Bones, his hustler cousin and alter ego.

"'Those people own the backbone and some of everything else in this country,'" Mingus has Billy Bones saying. "Even this chump Mingus's profession, which might be said to make whores out of musicians. . . . Now, Mingus, here's how to save yourself from depending on what rich punks think and critics say about jazz, true jazz, your work. By my reckoning a good musician has got to turn to pimpdom in order to be free and keep his soul straight. Jelly Roll Morton had seven girls I know of and that's the way he bought the time to write and study and incidentally got diamonds in his teeth and probably his asshole.'"

But in Mingus's case, pretensions to pimpdom and all-around badness were, I still think, a front as well as an exquisite cover. Mingus loved women too much to ever exploit them that way. He was forever falling in love, although he often pretended it was all a bore and a trap, so he wrote pieces like "What Love," which lyrically betrayed his kiss-and-tell romanticism. All the same, I have to bring up this cocky, macho swaggering so many black male musicians affect. It must've driven female geniuses like Lil Hardin, Mary Lou Williams and Melba Liston nuts.

The writerly me wants to plant either an exclamation point or a question mark at the end of that title so that it reads: "What Love!" or "What Love?" But Mingus, no slouch at wordslinging, left it unpunctuated. And now, decades later, I play the piece back and get the sweetest hit of all as it pours and swirls through the room and right out the window and back in again like the sigh of every sleepless lover who ever thought out loud in whispers. I'd put this swooning melody right up there with Monk's "'Round Midnight" as one of the most beautiful songs of the twentieth century.

I Can't Get Started _____

All the Mingus moments crowd into this, the only moment there is—

Mingus at noon in his all-white Charlie Chan suit and Panama hat, fat and resplendent, walking into the Ninth Circle with his beautiful wife Judy and their baby girl the summer I stopped off at New York before sailing to Europe on a Portuguese freighter with my head all ablaze with Mingus's muscular blues, "Nostalgia in Times Square"—

Mingus leaving the stand at the Minor Key on Dexter Boulevard in Detroit and making Dannie Richmond get behind his drum kit and play all by himself as a disciplinary measure for turning up at the gig late and drunk—

Mingus shrouded in cigarette smoke at the mike of San Francisco's Jazz Workshop (while pianist

Jane Getz looks on in her dark glasses and leopard-skin coat), telling the management he'll pick up the tab for one table of black patrons: "They don't like it 'cause I got a white girl on piano, so they can leave right now, I'll pay for their drinks!"—

Mingus's voice (again in the blaze of near-noon) on the telephone to his son Charles Mingus III, who's standing with me in the middle of his father's Third Avenue loft, and I can hear what Mingus is saying to his son: "Get Al Young outta there as fast as you can and don't let him see any of my papers or manuscripts!"—

Mingus on the phone again, seated beside me at the bar; the San Francisco gig is over and he's saying to someone at the other end: "OK, all right, that's cool, I've got an incurable disease anyway!"—

Mingus at the Ninety-second Street YW-YMHA, where I'm giving a poetry reading with Philip Appleman, and he and Sue Graham, on their way to a Stevie Wonder concert at Madison Square Garden, have stopped off to catch my portion of performance, which Mingus appears to be sleeping through with his head down and his hands folded in his lap, but at the end, when I approach him, he smiles gently and tells me: "That was pretty good."—

Mingus of "Alice's Wonderland" (also identifiable as "Diane" and the final, melting section of his "Self Portrait in Three Colors") is probably my favorite Mingus; the one who still has me picturing pigeons flying out of horns, swishing me with wingfalls of silence as they flap and rise straight up into other dimensions, maybe even the very bend in time Mingus is operating out of right now—

Mingus at the Village Vanguard, charging people admission to watch him rehearse the Jazz Workshop orchestra, to which Eric Dolphy has brought an alto sax playing buddy of his who's seated in the band with his postal worker uniform, soloing on "Orange Was the Color of Her Dress, then Blue Silk," which prompts Mingus to wave the fellow away and say: "We already got one Eric, we don't need no more Eric Dolphys—and besides, this song is about a chick I met nine years ago, and she wasn't sad like you're making her sound, man, she was a joy to be around!"—

Mingus at Monterey, it's September 1964, and Arl and I and my lawyer pal Gordon Lapides from Detroit and his girlfriend, the painter JoAnne Stoutemyer, have driven down to catch his all-star band and, sitting there in the glow of his tribute to Duke Ellington, I'm jarred into laughter when Mingus takes the microphone and says: "Duke, I do love you madly. I've stolen enough."—

Mingus on the PBS videotape, *A Duke Named Ellington*, chording and soloing on a piano made out of air as he explains how Ellington was an improvisational genius: "When he's playing accompaniment to the soloists, he never repeats his comp. Most piano players have one, maybe two voicings for a chord, which is very sad and a drag to me, because I've been lucky enough to play with Duke and with Art [Tatum] and Bud Powell; they never repeat their comp. Duke could sit down at the piano alone and, in twenty minutes or ten minutes, play you a symphony."—

Mingus in performance, getting that impish look of relief on his face as he signals to the band that it's time for a tempo change, which he always did whenever the tempo got to be too stiff or erect, or, as the astonishing Boston pianist and saxophonist Jaki Byard put it: "This is what made playing with Mingus a ball—his ability to relieve some of the unrelenting obligations to the soloist that can otherwise turn accompaniment into an endurance test."—

Mingus on the radio, Berkeley's KPFA with Phil Elwood, 1965: "How much does Fats Waller's family get while his records are being played? His family; not his publishers. His little boy killed himself. He was living in poverty; he was a great saxophone player, much like Sonny Rollins. He lived out on Jamaica, Long Island. And I saw the house, and I couldn't imagine a person as famous as that living that much in the ghetto-style poverty. I think he [Fats Waller] was respected all over the world. This is a mark on this society's invisible slavery."

Mingus, Mingus, Mingus, Mingus—

❖   ❖   ❖

FOR YEARS I'VE BEEN TRYING to say all this. The problem is I can't get started. I mean, I keep trying to whisper sweet-somethings in this crazy pony's ear while she's trotting and galloping and bucking me heavenward. But there's no way to either begin or end what I need to say about Charles Mingus.

That's why everybody's still working out Vernon Duke's "I Can't Get Started," isn't it? How many times have I held my breath and lingered in bumptious clubs or hushed halls while Mingus sweetened and deepened that good old ostinato bass line? Whether using it was going to punctuate "Blue Moon," "Heart and Soul," or "Big Girls Don't Cry," amateur guitarists and fumbling pianists like myself just dive right on into those comforting chords and pound away: C to A to D to G and back to C again. But Mingus, like the best of songwriters, could turn "Heart and Soul" into Art and Soul.

Right now, as my fingers click and glide over this wordy keyboard, I'm listening to the ghost of him perform "I Can't Get Started." The record is *Mingus Plays Piano: Spontaneous Compositions and Improvisations.*

And now, hours later, here he is on another album, *Wonderland*, playing "I Can't Get Started" a whole different way. This time he's got John Handy with him and, even though Booker Ervin's there too, it's pretty much Mingus, Richard Wyands and good old Dannie Richmond again on brushes.

Mingus made that record in front of a live

audience at the Nonagon Art Gallery in 1959. Probably half the people clapping on the record are gone from this world. This is a thought that also occurs to me when I watch Groucho Marx in those ancient "You Bet Your Life" reruns on T.V. Mingus's friend, saxophonist Buddy Collette, was the first black musician to play with the band for that show, which always struck me as funny.

It's funny to hear Mingus and John playing so close-knit and lovingly again. What a wonderful player John is! It's almost the end of the century and people are still humming and singing the solo he did on Mingus's tribute to Lester Young, "Goodbye Porkpie Hat," the same way tenor players still quote Illinois Jacquet's solo from Lionel Hampton's original "Flyin' Home."

What did Mingus think of the words his friend Joni Mitchell put to that piece? If Joni's hit didn't help haul Mingus and his work into pop consciousness, then what could?

"I cut eight albums with Mingus," John Handy says, "and this is what's remembered."

Then as now, John sounds as if he's playing from the tips of his toes right on up into the medulla oblongata and on up through the crown chakra. And the quizzical way Mingus is quoting "Ain't Gonna Study War No More" and "Stormy Weather" in his exquisitely plucked solo makes me remember I haven't breathed for an entire chorus.

On this version of "I Can't Get Started," Mingus _____ 161

and Handy sound placid, droll and, at the same time, wise and world-weary. Gary Giddins might've been right about jazz being a world-weary music.

It's true; it is hard to get started. How come? Maybe Mingus felt he couldn't get started because he was already way ahead of the world game when he arrived here in 1922. He even came by way of a retired army sergeant and a mother who wouldn't live to see him past his third month.

I'm thinking about how he started out on trombone. Since my own band days, I've always paid attention to how different instruments attracted different personalities. So I have to chuckle when I consider that trombone was Mingus's first choice. ("I hear the human voice when I hear that instrument," he often said.) Then he took up cello, because they needed one in the school orchestra and Britt Woodman egged him on. And finally Buddy Collette turned around and urged Mingus to try the double bass.

There it all is in a nutshell, or a bandshell, or maybe it's more like a set of nesting baskets—Mingus's three basic personalities, the same ones I can still pick up whenever I listen to him play. Play, not work.

❖   ❖   ❖

HERE MINGUS IS IN MY EAR right now, for instance, the serious jazz bassist, keeping time and knocking me

and the historic audience out with the deft, ballsy

tenderness of his strokes. He's the gentle bully of a
romantic who probably cut quite a figure in another
era, where passionate and tempered emotions alike
required eloquent if not elegant expression. All of
that deep feeling must've come out when he sat to
be the cellist and play those church gigs with his
violinist and pianist sisters Grace and Vivian. Perhaps this muted version of Mingus, growing up in a
household where jazz was forbidden, contributed
to the making of Mingus the coolster. Or perhaps
this tender tendency made possible such reflective
pieces as "Meditation on a Pair of Wire Cutters,"
"Goodbye Porkpie Hat," "Myself When I Am Real,"
"Celia," and countless other mood-drenched pieces.

Of course when we come back to the trombone,
to Mingus, Britt Woodman, Kid Ory, Eddie Bert,
Willie Dennis, J.J. Johnson, Kai Winding, Jimmy
Knepper, Slide Hampton, Charles Greenlee, Quen-
tin "Butter" Jackson and all the other trombonists he
ever had around him, there we touch base with the
jocular Mingus; the extrovert and prankster; the
trickster. That seems to be the side of him everybody loved to loathe and be awed by; the pain-in-
the-ass artist with a reputation for being mercurial
and dangerous.

Then as now, I only ever knew him as a volcanic
presence who seemed to know his time wasn't
long, and who thought he could never get started.

I'm riding that wild Mingusian horse again. You
might could call it Pegasus but, call it what you will,

MINGUS
MINGUS

it sounds and smells like the roaring-train facet of Mingus's diamond sound; purr and thunder, tiptoe and clickety-clackety—and whether I'm immersed in Times Square or time squared, I can always hear and feel and rush with it down and around the tracks of my years.

Janet Coleman has written frequently for *New York*, *The Village Voice*, *Vanity Fair*, *Mademoiselle*, *Book World*, and *Book Week*. She is also author of *The Compass: the Improvisational Theatre That Revolutionized American Comedy*. With her husband, David Dozer, she performs and writes for stage, screen, radio and television. She lives in Greenwich Village.

Al Young was born in 1939, a native of Mississippi who grew up in Detroit and the San Francisco Bay Area, where he has lived for most of his life. He is the award-winning author of several screenplays and more than 15 books, including *Heaven: Poems 1956–1990*, the novels *Sitting Pretty* and *Seduction by Light*, and the *Musical Memoirs Trilogy: Bodies & Soul*, *Kinds of Blue* and *Things Ain't What They Used To Be*. He travels extensively, lecturing and reading from his work, which has been widely translated.